PRIVATE
AND
PERSONAL

Praise for Carol Weston, *Girltalk*, and *For Girls Only*

"Carol Weston's writing is solid, sensible, and kind."
—Mary Pipher, Ph.D., author of *Reviving Ophelia*

"Wise, warm, witty . . . *Girltalk* is a must for every young woman's library."

—*YM*

"There are so many dumb advice books for girls that it's a pleasure to find one that really works. *For Girls Only* offers 'Wise Words, Good Advice' for the 10-and-up set. Carol Weston, advice columnist for *Girls' Life* magazine, does what many parents of adolescents cannot: She resists the inclination to drone on. Weston, herself the mother of two daughters, doesn't talk down to her young readers. She doesn't preach. And she doesn't come off as a prude. As a result, her advice about school, family, and friends is appealing to an age group that very much wants to know the answers but automatically tunes out parental lectures."
—Katy Kelly, *USA Today*

"Carol Weston is one of the few writers who can quote Cindy Crawford, Goethe, Mother Teresa, Billie Holiday, Francis Bacon, and Tom Cruise in one slim volume and make it work. *For Girls Only* is a quotation book with appeal for teenagers and parents . . . absolutely the right approach for teenage girls."
—Nancy Gilson, *Columbus Dispatch*

"Here's a totally helpful read that's packed with clever quotes by everyone from Buddha to Bill Cosby. Weston puts a new spin on some age-old advice, and you come out being able to handle all your probs brilliantly."
—*All About You!* Magazine

Look for These Other Books by
Carol Weston

FOR GIRLS ONLY:
WISE WORDS, GOOD ADVICE

GIRLTALK:
ALL THE STUFF YOUR SISTER NEVER TOLD YOU

THE DIARY OF MELANIE MARTIN:
OR HOW I SURVIVED
MATT THE BRAT, MICHELANGELO,
AND THE LEANING TOWER OF PIZZA

PRIVATE
AND
PERSONAL

Questions and Answers for Girls Only

● ● ● ● ●

Carol Weston

🎀 HarperTrophy®
A Division of HarperCollinsPublishers

Some of these letters were originally published in *Girls' Life* magazine. Grateful acknowledgment is made to the editors for permission to reprint adaptations of that material.

Library of Congress Catalog Card Number: 99-96353
ISBN 0-380-81025-5

First Harper Trophy edition, 2000
❖
Visit us on the World Wide Web!
www.harperchildrens.com

For every girl who thought she was alone

What's Inside

A Few Thank-Yous

Thank you Elise Howard, A#1 editor, for knowing when to push and when to pull and for caring about girls as much as I do.

Thank you Laura Peterson, ideal agent, for your spirit and savvy.

Thank you *Girls' Life*, for permission to reprint many "Dear Carol" letters, and to Karen Bokram, who handed me a dream job. Thanks also to Kelly White and Georgia Wilson, for your help with my "Help!" column.

Thanks to all the Yalies who lent me their insight and energy: Evie Gurney, Amber Gross, Mike Wolmetz, Ann Zeidner, and Erin Arruda.

Thanks to the New York, Ohio, and Colorado students who commented on different sections of this book: Tara Rodman, Sarah Jeffrey, Kyla Brennan, Amanda Katz, Cassie Jenkins, Leni Kirschenbaum.

Thanks to Marybeth Weston Lobdell, for being my first editor and only mom.

Thanks to Lauren Westbrook, Ph.D.; Max Kahn, M.D.; Adam Romoff, M.D.; Liz Pennisi, R.N.; and Susan Tew of the Alan Guttmacher Institute, for answering *my* questions.

Thanks to all the girls who have ever written me. I hope you're finding your way!

Last but not least, thanks especially and always to my family: Robert, Elizabeth, and Emme Ackerman for critiquing my chapters but taking me as I am. I love you!

The Beginning

So how's it going? Fine . . . with occasional moments of misery?

You've come to the right book. Sit down and get comfortable.

Ever since I wrote *Girltalk*, I've been getting female mail. Because of my "Help!" column in *Girls' Life*, I get more letters than ever. Some are scrawled in pencil on looseleaf; some are in pink ink on kitty-cat stationery; some are penned or typed or e-mailed. Many are marked "Rush" or "Urgent" or "Please Open Right Away." Week after week, month after month, year after year, I've been mailing off answers and throwing away questions.

But deep down, I must have always known I would write this book, because whenever I came across a letter that was particularly poignant or painful or funny or typical, I didn't just answer it and throw it away. I stashed the letter, and sometimes a copy of my response, in my file cabinet.

Cut to fifteen years later and—my filing cabinet was about to explode!

I started making piles. I'm-shy piles. My-sister-is-annoying piles. Why-aren't-I-popular? piles. Will-I-ever-develop? piles. Will-I-ever-stop-developing? piles. I-wish-I-had-a-boyfriend piles. I'm-sick-of-my-boyfriend piles.

My tables and chairs were soon covered with letters. I felt overwhelmed but also awestruck. Here was a reflection of what was on the minds and in the hearts of girls. Here was a mix of mostly middle-school letters that showed precisely what girls wonder and worry about. What girls want to know.

I chose one or two letters from each small pile and several from each big pile. I shortened letters, cleaned up spelling, changed or omitted names, and included answers. But I didn't make any letters up. Didn't have to.

Now these letters and pages are in your hands.

You can read this book straight through. Or you can skip around. Or you and a friend can take turns reading questions aloud and comparing your answers with mine. You don't agree with each other or me? Excellent! That should spark conversation.

I've always felt honored to be trusted by so many girls. I started writing for teens when I was a teen, and I feel lucky that I'm still at it years later, and that I now have two daughters of my own to love and teach and learn from.

The middle years can be hard. You're between grade school and high school, between being a kid and being a woman. You know so much, but you're still full of hard-to-ask questions. I hope this book answers some of your questions and also puts your problems in perspective.

My earlier books are full of everything I wanted girls to know. *Girltalk: All the Stuff Your Sister Never Told You* has excerpts from my own diaries and information for older teens.

For Girls Only includes quotations from more than 450 famous men and women, from Buddha to Oprah, Aesop to Anne Frank, Shakespeare to Cher.

Private and Personal has more of you in it. It's not what *I* want you to know. It's what *you* want to know.

If your brother or boyfriend wants to take a peek, go ahead, let him. But I have, once again, written this book for girls only.

And for you especially.

So why muddle through middle school?

It helps to hear from girls who are going through what you're going through. And it helps to hear from a sage and sensible sort who not only survived the Age of Embarrassment, but who's sticking around to offer a helping hand.

Me!

Turn the page!

OH ME OH MY

● ● ● ● ●

Everyone says to be yourself, but that can be hard because you're still figuring out who you are. Do you think about what you enjoy doing, what you're good at, why you hang out with the people you hang out with? How are you like and unlike your friends? When I moved in the middle of sixth grade, I felt more self-conscious than self-confident, and I wanted to blend in and be accepted. I've gotten bolder as I've gotten older, and now instead of just fitting in, I'm happy to stand out. I like working on goals that matter to me and caring about people who care about me. I like being who I am.

I hope you like being—and becoming—who you are.

Dear Carol,
Sometimes I want to be younger, sometimes I want
to be older, and the rest of the time I feel caught
between both worlds. I can't tell anyone because I
don't have the courage.

Confused

Dear Confused,
It took courage to tell me. And I'm here to tell
you that feeling confused is totally normal—
especially now. Of course you want to do kid
stuff. Of course you want to do teenage stuff. It's
fun to do cartwheels and it's fun to slow dance. If
you talk to a close friend, you may find that she
understands just how you feel and has even felt
the same way.

Dear Carol,
I have a strange problem. Sometimes I have a posi-
tive attitude about myself and feel great. Other times
it's the exact opposite. I have a negative attitude and
feel bad.

Positive/Negative

Dear Positive/Negative,
Sounds human to me. Everyone's confidence
goes up and down. To strengthen your self-
esteem, do things that make you proud. Work to
pull up grades, join activities to build skills and

deepen friendships, volunteer for a cause, and find time to do what you do well—whether it's drawing, writing, or running races. Try to learn a lot about one subject, too, such as sea otters, shipwrecks, or Van Gogh. Becoming an expert in a field can help you feel on top of things.

Dear Carol,
I really need your help. I don't know who I am. Am I a tough girl dressed in black or a kind little girl?
Split Personalities

Dear S.P.,
Nobody is 100 percent tough or 100 percent kind. Different people and situations bring out different sides of you. You're still changing and growing. Perhaps you're a mix of tough and kind and proud and modest and athletic and artistic and serious and fun. Nothing wrong with that!

Dear Carol,
I'm afraid I'm growing up too fast. I feel bad for my mom because I am the youngest. She treats me like a baby, and I don't want to hurt her feelings.
Growing Up

Dear Growing Up,
It can be bittersweet for parents to watch their little darlings outgrow childhood clothes, books, and games. But moms also feel proud of daughters and sons as they strike out on their own. In lucky families, children grow into adult friends.

Just as your mom loved you as a baby, toddler, and little kid, she will love you as a young adult. And you'll never outgrow hugs and conversation.

Dear Carol,
I am 12 and I'm afraid to grow up. I just know I'll miss being a kid. I try my best to think how great it will be to be an adult, but one more year and it's all over.

Female Peter Pan

Dear F.P.P.,
What's all over? Childhood doesn't end abruptly the moment you turn 13 or get your period or have your first bra or date or kiss. Growing up is gradual. And you'll always be you. Enjoy being 12, but relax—your parents aren't about to kick you out of the nest or make you start buying and cooking all your food or buying and washing all your clothes. As for how great it is to be an adult, here are three things to look forward to: no homework, no tests, and you usually get to pick your roommate.

Dear Carol,
I'm sort of a goody-goody. I get straight A's and have never really broken the rules. Lately I've been tempted to do wild things like dye my hair, pierce my body, or even steal and stuff. It's wrong, but I'm tired of being Miss Perfect.

Miss Perfect

Dear Miss Perfect,
I'd rather hang out with a smart person than a thief any day. Feel proud, not ashamed, of your grades, and remember that the kids who tease you probably wish they could bring home report cards like yours. I understand your urge to go wild, but I doubt you'd feel happier if your hair were green or eyebrows were pierced. How else can you express yourself? What do you like to do when you have free time? Get involved in different after-school activities, throw a party, and figure out ways to break out of your mold without breaking the rules.

Dear Carol,
I have a problem. I judge people by their looks. I know it's not fair and I try to stop, but how can I?
Judge

Dear Judge,
At least you're honest! Lots of people judge by looks, which is why it's important to wash your hair, wear clean clothes, and check the mirror before dashing out the door. Trying to look decent in the morning shows self-respect, and it's fine to develop that in yourself and appreciate it in others. But you're right that it's not fair to judge solely by looks. People can't help it if their bodies or noses are big or small, and not everyone chooses to wear or can afford name-brand clothes. Part of getting older is learning to see

beyond surfaces. Just as you're learning to judge adults more by how they act than how they look, you can develop that radar with kids. Appearance should be just one of many clues you use to figure out others. Besides, many real friends talk on the phone and on-line—where looks don't matter.

Dear Carol,
I spend a lot of time on the Internet—too much. I get angry when my mom tells me to get off the computer. Help!

Caught In The Net

Dear C.I.T.N.,
Once you turn on the computer, it can be hard to turn it off. Since you know you're overdoing it and you don't like when your mom tells you to sign off, start telling yourself when enough is enough. This is not easy, but it's what adults do. Since nobody tells me, "Carol, it's 11:30—don't you think it's time to go to bed?" or "Carol, you *already* had a chocolate truffle," or "Carol, you've been on-line for an hour!" I have to be responsible and "parent" myself. And I do a pretty good job of it—most of the time. You, too, can start "parenting" yourself instead of waiting for your mom to nag you and then resenting her for it.

Here are more ideas: Finish your homework and dinner before signing on; log on from, say, 8 to 9 only; decide that for every hour you spend on-line, you'll put in an hour of ball playing or reading; set up the computer in a less inviting space; before you log on, set a timer or alarm clock for when you want to log off; make a list of things you can do if you don't plug in; finally, let your mom know you're changing your ways, but also offer her surfing lessons so she can see how you use the Web for research. (Research—not shoe shopping or quiz taking!)

Dear Carol,
I suck my thumb. Only my mom and dad know. I have tried everything from socks on my hand to just plain stopping. The worst part is that I have braces.
                                                                    Big Baby

Dear Big Baby,
Habits are hard to break! I'll let you in on a secret. I sucked my thumb—and worried about it—for too long, too. I tried going to bed with a glove on, applying Band-Aids, and putting bad-tasting polish on my thumbnail. I tried allowing myself to suck my thumb only in my room and only during certain times. Somehow I finally got to the point where I wanted to break the habit more than I wanted to suck my thumb. (I think I was petrified that I'd get found out at a sleep-over.) Since you have braces to straighten your teeth, you have an extra incentive. And since

your mom and dad know, consider asking them for a small reward if you can go five days without thumb-sucking. Then find a mitten and a stress ball and start counting. But forgive yourself, too—you're not a big baby. And you're not the only person trying to break a habit.

Dear Carol,
I really like dolls. One time I took one with me to a store and the cutest boys walked in. The next day it was all over school.

Twelve Going On Three

Dear Twelve,
Oops, you must have turned a few colors. But put it behind you. Truth is, most people are so preoccupied with themselves (the zits on their foreheads, the holes in their tights, the croaks in their voices) that they aren't as focused on you as you might think. At home, enjoy your chosen pastimes. At school, hold your head high and don't worry about yesterday's news. There are millions of Barbies (Beanie Babies, Furbies, etc.), so it's not as if you alone have a thing for them.

Dear Carol,
I have this reputation of not liking boys, but now I like one. If I go out with him, my family will probably find out and my sisters and brothers will laugh at me.

Changing

Dear Changing,
Sooner or later, your family will discover that you've been revising your opinion of the opposite sex. Some parents and siblings take things in stride, others tease, others flip out. You can be discreet about your feelings, but you don't have to pretend you're in grade school forever. Whether you confide in your mom or sibling or not, you are allowed to grow up.

Dear Carol,

I am 14 and I have a boyfriend who is sweet, caring, considerate, a good listener and a good conversationalist. We've been going together for two months. We were friends first. This boy respects my feelings and doesn't pressure me (except about schoolwork). There's only one problem. My mom would go crazy if she found out. I want to tell her, and he wants me to tell her, but I don't know how. See, I'm not supposed to talk to boys on the phone and anytime I mention a boy, my mom goes nuts. So can you please pretty please with sugar on top help me tell my mother about my boyfriend?

Mom Won't Let Me Grow Up

Dear M.W.L.M.G.U.,
Sounds like you're growing up whether your mom will let you or not. Yours is a tricky question because you don't feel right about not telling her, but if you do tell, you don't exactly expect her to give you her blessings. Advice? Do

not rush to say that you've been keeping a two-month-old secret. Do consider saying, "Mom, hear me out. I want to be as honest with you as possible because I like being able to talk with you. I want you to know that there is this guy I like who likes and respects me . . ." If you can already hear her going "crazy" and "nuts," then think about this a little longer. It's your decision, your risk.

Dear Carol,
I have created an image for myself that I do not like. I've tried to change, but it's hard. I put gobs of make-up on. I smoked so a guy would like me. I stole one of my best friend's boyfriends. Sign me—

Bad Girl

Dear B.G.,
How does all that make you feel? Lousy, right? Well, behind the makeup and smoke, there's a good person afraid to come out. Let her out! Yes, change is hard—for you to do and for others to recognize. But make the effort. Since you no longer want to play the part of a way-cool tough girl, stop playing dress-up and think about how you do want to come off. Go to school with little or no makeup. Smile a little more. Ask friendly questions and give compliments, even if it feels fake at first. Join an activity. Praise yourself instead of telling yourself you are bad. As for

cigarettes, hands off! If you smoke, you run the risk of becoming a *smoker*, and why pick up an unhealthy, expensive, addictive habit? And no more boyfriend stealing—girlfriends are too valuable.

Dear Carol,

I feel sort of stupid writing this, but when I learned there was no Santa Claus, I was heartbroken. Christmas Eve used to feel so magical. My mom says you have to have faith, but having faith isn't going to make reindeer fly or Santa come down my chimney. Is there such a thing as magic that's not made up?

Disappointed

Dear Disappointed,

It may be disappointing to realize that reindeer don't fly and Santa doesn't shimmy down the chimney, but look at it this way: Isn't it amazing to think of how hard parents work to delight kids? Santa may be pretend, but he'll be making merry a hundred years from now. That is a fact. And I think it's kind of . . . magical.

Dear Carol,

I need advice on how to keep my room clean. I want to get contacts, but my parents won't let me unless I keep my room clean. I'm always feeling trapped in my own room.

Trapped

Dear Trapped,

If you took a look at my office, you'd know that neat-and-tidy is not my strong suit. Nonetheless, here goes: When you feel trapped, force yourself to start digging through and sorting out. Don't get overwhelmed—get started, bit by bit. Put on an upbeat CD and keep organizing until the music is done. Start with the stuff on your floor and/or desk. Make three piles: put away, throw away, and give away. Same thing with drawers: Dump a drawer on the floor, then put away, throw away, or give away. Take your clothes out of your closet and if there are things you don't like or don't wear, give them to someone younger or to a church, synagogue, or shelter. Keep at it all afternoon or for an hour a day for a week, and you'll be astounded by how much better your room looks and you feel. If you think someone in your family would be supportive, not critical, invite him or her to help you arrange books, label drawers, clear out clutter, or even give your room an inspection. Try to get in the lifelong habit of doing a little daily or weekly cleanup and of hanging up clothes and putting away papers—even after you've gotten those contact lenses. But give yourself a break, too. Getting organized comes more naturally to some people than to others.

Speaking Up

Dear Carol,
I'm shy and I can't stand it. I can never think of any-
thing to say to people I've just met or to adults. I'm
worried that people will think I'm stuck-up or boring.
Since I'm so quiet, I hardly ever get any attention and
when I do talk, my voice gets shaky.

Shy Not Snobby

Dear Shy Not Snobby,
Many confident women started as shy girls. Since
you crave attention and don't want to be mistaken for a snob, start speaking up. When you
meet someone new, comment on what you two
are doing. "Isn't this an exciting game/beautiful
wedding/delicious picnic?" The easiest way to
break the ice is to give a compliment: "Nice
shirt," "Great necklace," "You have such a good
accent in French," "I like the poem you wrote."
Most people like to talk about themselves, so ask
questions: "What's your dog's name?" "Have you
ever read this book?" "Did you have a good weekend?" "How's field hockey going?" If you want
people to show interest in you, show interest
in them. Adults are usually charmed when kids
or teens ask polite questions. Practice on easy
people. When your aunt says, "How's school?"
instead of shrugging, tell her some little story,
then ask, "How's work?" She won't say, "None of

your business"; she'll be pleased that you cared enough to ask. And when someone tells you a story? Don't just sit there. Say, "That is hysterical!" or "You must have been worried," or whatever else fits the moment. Little by little, you'll be speaking up naturally and getting others to talk, and that shakiness in your voice will disappear.

Dear Carol,
I'm a huge pushover. I constantly worry about what others think of me and can never get the courage to stand up for myself without feeling guilty. I get so flustered, I want to run and hide.
Pushed Over Too Many Times

Dear Pushed,
A lot of girls are too accommodating. If you speak up, what are you guilty of? Having an opinion? Being an individual? You don't approve of everybody and everybody won't approve of you and that's all right. To become more assertive, start speaking your mind in places where you feel safe—at home or in your favorite class. Dinner out is always pizza because that's your brother's first choice? Say, "We had pizza last time. How about Chinese?" You'll find that it feels good to express yourself.

Dear Carol,
When I talk to people, I can't look at them in the eye. But I don't want to be known as an insecure person because I'm not.

Eye Dropper

Dear Eye Dropper,
Ten points for realizing that in America, meeting people's eyes is generally considered a sign of warmth, courtesy, and confidence. Tomorrow, try to maintain eye contact with three people who don't intimidate you. Forget your crush—try your bus driver, librarian, or friend's mom. Make a game of really noticing the color and shape of their eyes, then silently applaud yourself for your efforts. Next thing you know, instead of looking down and mumbling, "hi," you'll be making eye contact *and* conversation. Bonus: People will trust you more and treat you with more respect.

Dear Carol,
I repeat myself so much. I'm always forgetting who I told what. I'll tell my friend something, and she'll say, "I know—you told me already." I think I'm starting to annoy my friends. Help!

Repeating Myself

Dear Repeating,
Conversation should be part talking, part listening. When you tell a friend something, you're

not just telling a story, you're supposed to be listening to her response, whether it's laughter, horror, questions, advice, or a story of her own. Open your ears as well as your mouth. If you say, "How can I tell my mom that I want to buy a bra?" and your friend has already given you three suggestions, then yes, she'll be miffed that her words never landed. We all repeat ourselves once in a while while while, so don't become paranoid or closemouthed. But do be more attentive. Feeling unsure? Cover yourself by saying, "I told you he called, right?" before plunging into a saga.

Dear Carol,
I have a big problem: I swear. I used to do it only once in a while. Now I do it everywhere and in front of everyone and I need to stop before I get into big trouble.

Sweared Out

Dear Sweared Out,
Recognizing a problem is the first step toward solving it. You're smart to want to stop because people who constantly swear come off as rude, not cool. When the urge strikes, try saying another word, maybe even a made-up one. Reward yourself when you've gone all morning without swearing, and consider enlisting a sibling or close friend to help you watch your words. Since you would like to be more eloquent, keep reaching for the right word—not the swear word.

Dear Carol,
I lie too much! I've been told to be myself, but I always feel I have to impress people. This summer at camp, I was just bursting with lies. I'm pretty good at it, too. People almost always believe me.

Liar

Dear Liar,
Making friends is more important than impressing people. You say that people almost always believe you. That means that sometimes they see right through you—and your claim to be an actor's girlfriend or musician's niece. Friendships thrive on trust, so make today the day you start connecting with people instead of merely holding court. If you do catch yourself exaggerating, just backtrack. Say, "I didn't literally buy ten outfits—more like two."

Feeling Anxious or Afraid

Dear Carol,
My family just moved and I'm going to a new school. People liked me at my old school, but I don't know anyone here, and I don't know how to act.

New In Town

Dear New In Town,
Who says you have to act? You made friends in your old school, and you'll do it again. Be

yourself—your friendliest self. Your nervousness is understandable, but if you say, "hi," smile a lot, introduce yourself, and listen well, you'll find your footing. It also helps to join after-school activities (e.g., chorus, student council, soccer) or community activities (e.g., cleaning a park, helping at a soup kitchen, or participating in a sport outside school). Working at things you like will put you in contact with people you like who will like you.

Dear Carol,

I'm notorious for being annoying. I like it, I'm known for it, and it fits me. The only thing is, my friends don't like it at all. I'm moving, and I'm worried that I won't make friends with my weird personality. Sometimes I'm calm, but mostly I'm like the Energizer bunny. Is that bad?

Energizer Bunny

Dear Energizer Bunny,
It's good to be energetic and content with yourself. It's not so good to grate on friends. Since you are starting fresh, can you tone down a bit so you can make the most of your opportunity to make new friends? Start noticing when others are having fun with you versus when they are tuning you out. Your personality and behavior aren't givens, after all; you do have some control. If you do think you've tried and still can't control your own behavior as much as you want,

consider asking your doctor if there might be a physical cause to your bouncy behavior or excess energy.

Dear Carol,
My best friend is an only child. Her aunt lives in Florida and her family invited me to go there on vacation with them. (They go every spring.) My parents said OK, but this is the problem and I know it sounds dumb: I don't know if I'm up to going. The thought of a week away scares me. What if I get homesick?

Homebody

Dear Homebody,
Homesickness isn't a disease that would land you in the hospital. It's more like a short period of feeling blue and wistful and missing your mom and dad. Talk to your parents about your feelings and fears. It's natural to be nervous, but while weighing the pros and cons, keep in mind that you're considering going with a friend to Florida—not a stranger to Siberia. Ask your friend what she likes most about vacationing there—collecting seashells? counting pelicans? catching waves? eating ice cream?—and try to get yourself psyched. No one is going to force you to go, but there's a lot to be said for saying yes to memorable opportunities. You can always pack your favorite stuffed animal and you can phone home from down South. You can even ask your parents to write you a note to open for each day you're away.

Dear Carol,
I feel terrible! I am almost 13 years old and am petrified of shots. When I last went to get a small shot, I fainted. If I even hear my friends talking about anything internal, I feel sick and light-headed.

Terrified

Dear Terrified,

A career in medicine may not be for you. Look, shots aren't fun, but it's better to survive a quick shot than die of a disease. Next time you're about to be pricked, try my trick: Look away and do a word game with yourself. If the nurse's name is Jessica, come up with a girl's name for each letter in her name, i.e. Jennifer, Elizabeth, Samantha, Stephanie, Isabelle, Cassie—chances are the shot will be over before you even get to Anna, and if not, start over with boys' names. (Confession: I do this at the dentist's and gynecologist's, too. I also count backward from 100 by 3s.) Time will help. I, for one, used to be a lot more afraid of spiders and bees than I am now. (Not that I'm about to become an entomologist or anything.) While most childhood phobias do go away on their own, if you have one that really bothers you when you're older, talk to a doctor or counselor about it.

Dear Carol,
I have a problem. I am such a worrier. I worry that someone's going to break into my house, that I am

going to get a heart attack, anything. It makes me sick to my stomach when I worry so much. I have been to the doctor's twice to see if I had an ulcer. I don't.

Worrying

Dear Worrying,
It must be hard to worry so much, but you are young and you can change. Here are two ideas: Set aside ten minutes each day to worry intensely and then, that's it, time's up. Or write a daily list of your ten big worries along with ten reasons why they'd probably never happen. Your goal is not to let worrying keep you from enjoying your life. If you can't stop the fretting on your own, talk to your school counselor or have your parents make an appointment with a good therapist, psychologist, or psychiatrist who can help you get to the root of your anxiety. Getting involved in group activities (sports, theater, gymnastics, computer club) is also a great way to live in the moment.

Dear Carol,
This might sound silly but it's true: I'm afraid to die. I think about it mostly at night. I look to each birthday with dread knowing that the older I get, the sooner I'll die. I really love my grandma, and I hate to think someday she'll die. I've already talked to my parents. Please give me advice.

Scared to Death

Dear Scared to Death,

Few of us look forward to the inevitable, but the good news is that you probably have decades and decades and decades ahead. When it comes to death, many people find comfort in religion. Many try to glean wisdom from philosophers and writers (from Plato to Camus to Woody Allen). And many just go into a happy, healthy denial and do their best to make the most of each day and not give the grim reaper much thought. If morbid thoughts are keeping you awake at night, say to yourself, "Self, now cut it out. I know what you're up to, and I won't go there." Then think about your crush, favorite song, best friend, last vacation, or the sound of the surf, or just picture yourself floating on a cloud.

I wish you and I were both immortal. We're not, but life is long and while you're here, you might as well figure out what makes you feel good, how to love and be loved, and how to help others. It's fine to be a deep person who ponders the big picture; but it's also OK to turn on some tunes and get into living. My suggestion: Bobby McFerrin's "Don't Worry, Be Happy."

Dear Carol,
I hate to admit it, but I'm afraid of ghosts and aliens so I'm afraid to go upstairs by myself. I'm 11 and I still sleep with a night-light. What should I do?

Fraidy Cat

Dear Fraidy Cat,
Forgive yourself. Eleven isn't thaaaaaat old. But push yourself, too. Put on lights and loud music and say to yourself, "Silly me. I know there's no such thing as ghosts and aliens!" Instead of being scared to climb the steps, and scolding yourself for your cowardice, climb the steps and compliment yourself for your bravery. If it helps, whistle or picture yourself holding your mom's hand as you climb. Then keep your mind busy by saying, "Yay me! I'm doing it! Up up up I go! I am the best!" When you reach the top, you'll feel genuinely proud.

Dear Carol,
I have wanted to sing for most of my life. I have tried to sing in front of people I do not know, but I am too afraid. How can I learn not to be afraid of what I want to do?

Singer

Dear Singer,
Fear silences too many of us, so do your best to get gutsier. Take lessons and practice in front of your teacher and develop confidence in your voice. Whom do you find least intimidating? Your grandmother? A friend's mom? Tell them singing is important to you and you'd like to sing them one song. Since you have a gift, share it. Since you have a goal, pursue it.

Dear Carol,
I'm applying to boarding schools and am about to go on interviews. My friends aren't doing this. I need tips!

Anxiety Attack

Dear Anxiety Attack,
Interviews make everybody nervous. But whether you are applying to get into a school or to get a job, an interview is not a one-way street. It's the school's chance to check you out as well as your chance to check the school out. It's everyone's chance to see if you're a good match. To up your odds of getting accepted, prepare your questions and anticipate theirs. Practice aloud with a friend or parent. If asked, "What's your weak point?" say "I hate to give up on a project once I've begun," not "I'm compulsive and never know when to quit." If asked, "Why do you want to come here?" explain why—and don't say because your first choice turned you down or you hear it's a great party school.

On interview day, come early. Be neatly and conservatively dressed (no nose rings!). Shake hands firmly, maintain eye contact, sit up straight, and use complete sentences—with as few "likes," "you knows," and "ums" as possible. Toot your horn, but not too loudly, and discuss what you can offer the school, not just what you hope to gain. Finally, follow up with a thank-you note. Good luck!

Dear Carol,
I know this boy who says he would like to hurt some-
one. He is mean to animals. I know that his father
hunts and that means he owns guns. With all the
school shootings, I'm scared. What should I do?
                                        Freaked Out

Dear Freaked Out,
Is this boy a big-mouthed bully or a menace to
society? You shouldn't have to be the one to make
that judgment. Tell a parent exactly what you told
me. Or type an anonymous note on plain paper
to your teacher or principal or both. You wouldn't
be landing the boy in jail; you'd be alerting an
adult about a worry that is too big for you. Ask to
keep your name out of things, then sleep well
knowing that you've done what you could.

Dear Carol,
I'm afraid to go outside after dark because I'm afraid
of kidnappers. When I'm lying in bed trying to get to
sleep, I have to pull the covers over my head. I'm
afraid to talk to my friends because they might laugh
and call me a baby or a chicken.
                                              Afraid
P.S. The reason I'm afraid is because my mom's friend
was kidnapped and killed.

Dear Afraid,
Wow. That's quite a P.S. What a tragedy for your
mom and her friend's family! No wonder you get

scared. If you tell your friends what you told me, they won't laugh. And talking to friends, parents, even a counselor will help you learn to be brave while still being cautious. Your anxiety is completely understandable, and in some situations, very smart. But you don't want to spend the rest of your evenings indoors. So it's time to control your fears rather than let them control you.

Do play it safe and stay alert. Don't walk alone. Don't hitchhike. Never let a stranger lure you into his car—even if he offers a gift or asks you to help him look for his lost dog or says that your parents asked him to pick you up. At home, lock the doors behind you. On the Internet, don't give out your number or address or password. On the phone, don't volunteer that you are alone. And if, God forbid, someone ever did try to force you to go with him, scream, "Let me go! I don't know you!" or "Help!" or "Call 911." If you just shout, "Stop it!" or "Leave me alone," a passerby might think you're arguing with your father or boyfriend and might not realize you're in trouble. For an extra sense of security, talk to your parents about getting an alarm system, or take kick-boxing or a self-defense course. And remember, despite scary headlines and news reports, the world is full of more good people than bad.

Feeling Different

Dear Carol,
I come from a different country, and I feel ashamed.
Ashamed

Dear Ashamed,
Right now you may wish you could blend into the crowd. But while it's fine to be a pea in a pod, I think it's even cooler to be a kumquat. Or fig. Or mango. Or pumpkin. It's not easy to switch from feeling shame to feeling pride, but try. What would a tourist like best about your country? What would a historian find most interesting? Is there a regional dish that you know how to cook that others might find delicious? Start peeking at the bright side of being different and please know that lots of girls and guys feel out of sync—even ones who were born around the corner.

Dear Carol,
I live in Hawaii and my family travels a lot. People ask all sorts of dumb questions when they find out I'm from Hawaii. "Do you speak a different language?" "Do you go surfing?" "Can you do the hula?" (No, no, and no.) It makes me so angry. How can I control my temper?

Hawaiian Not Martian

Dear Hawaiian,
You can't change strangers, but you can change your attitude. Most offenders are probably just trying to make conversation and many would simply like to know more about your home state. Instead of yelling at them, educate them. Tell them what you'd like them to know about yourself and Hawaii.

Dear Carol,
I'm rich. I live in a mansion. Most of my clothes are fancy dresses. My friends like being in my house more than they like me. I'm embarrassed about our richness, but I don't know how to tell my parents.
Sick Of Being Rich

Dear Sick Of Being Rich,
Try not to define yourself by your wealth. You wrote, "I'm rich." But are you also funny, smart, musical, athletic? Think of your wealth as an extra instead of an obstacle. Studies show that people who value relationships tend to feel more satisfied than people who value stuff, and you may be lucky enough to have both—friends and things. Sure, friends may like your house (or pool or pool table), but I bet they also like you. Talk with them about your feelings. Talk to your mom, too. Tell her you appreciate the fancy clothes, but you want to dress like your friends and could she please take you shopping for jeans and T-shirts?

Dear Carol,
I'm a little poor. Not like on-the-streets poor, but my family (my mom and I) can't afford a lot of things. My father is supposed to pay child support, but he doesn't. I'm a kid who thinks like a grown-up sometimes. Like, I know how much everything costs. I do have lots of stuff so I guess I'm lucky. But I still want a new swimsuit that fits (mine fits OK but my breasts stick out a little) and, you guessed it, I want a computer. We even shop sales and garage sales.

Poor

Dear P.,
Even people with lots of money shop sales and garage sales because why pay $100 for a coat if you can find one for $40—or $5? I'm also a big believer in (and wearer of) hand-me-downs because they save me time and money, and recycling is good for all of us. But it must be frustrating to feel short on cash when some kids have extra. A new swimsuit may be within your grasp, while a new computer may be harder to pull off. Is there a computer you can use at your school or library? Does your mom know someone with an older daughter who can pass clothes and books to you? Can you make money by running errands, baby-sitting, or being a mother's helper? Keep your grades up and you may be able to go to college on scholarship. For now, hang in there and stay aware of all that you do have.

Dear Carol,
A lot of my friends love to baby-sit, but I have a problem with little kids. I baby-sit this one kid, and I am always doing mean stuff to him or yelling at him. I really hate doing it to him but I just can't seem to stop. I haven't baby-sat for him in a while, and I don't want to because I hate hurting him.

Needs Help

Dear Needs,
Better to accept that baby-sitting is not for you than to say yes and then be mean to the child. If the family asks you to sit again, say you can't or say you realize you just don't have the patience for baby-sitting. No one ever said baby-sitting was easy. It's a big responsibility to be in charge of children's physical and emotional well-being (and some kids are more difficult than others). You're still young, too, so give yourself credit for recognizing that you aren't ready to take care of someone younger. There are other ways to make money: walking dogs, mowing lawns, delivering papers, house-sitting. Years from now, if you have children of your own, I hope you will read up and take classes on how to be the best mother you can be.

Dear Carol,
I am what you could call starstruck. I always dream about meeting certain actors and actresses. I don't want to be obsessed, but I really want to meet

famous celebrities, and I don't know how to tell myself that it will never happen. Why can't I be like everyone else and like the boy next door?

Starstruck

Dear Starstruck,
Stars shine brightest in magazines and interviews. In real life, celebs have to brush and floss just like the rest of us. That said, many girls like to read up on the rich and famous. Which is fine—unless you're waking up miserable because you aren't a certain actor's best friend or main squeeze. If it's no longer fun to be a fan, get busier with your here and now. Take up a new sport or instrument. Start a monthly book club with friends and maybe even their moms. Take an acting class and if your community has a theater, audition. You may be a star yourself someday—but you'll still have to brush and floss! As for the boy next door, perhaps you don't yet feel ready for the roller coaster of real romance. And that's fine.

Dear Carol,
I'm just starting to be invited to parties and I'm a little nervous because I am hearing-impaired and I don't like having to say "What?" and "Could you repeat that?" and "Sorry, I didn't catch your name," when I first meet people. I have hearing aids and I wear my hair over them. The girls I'm tight with know I'm hearing-impaired, but I don't like telling the whole world.

Hearing-Impaired

Dear H.I.,
Lots of girls and guys are uncomfortable when they first start going to parties, but it's understandable that you are extra self-conscious. Some parties are so loud that nobody can hear anything. Ask a friend to make introductions for you and help you wade through a few initial conversations. Push through your nervousness, and if someone seems nice, say, "Let's go over here where I can hear you better." Get conversations going in the kitchen or hallway or outside, away from the din and music. While some middle-school kids do judge on superficials, high school is around the corner, and by then, most people recognize—and accept—that we all have our differences and distinctions. By the way, on-line, you can enjoy parties in print by telling friends to log on at a certain time and perhaps by setting up buddy lists and trading instant messages.

Dear Carol,
I've heard about college students going on junior-year-abroad programs and I was wondering if you know of any programs for high-school students. I get good grades and I think my parents would let me go. My friends might think it's weird, though.

Curious

Dear Curious,
There are programs for students of all ages. I spent a month in southern France the summer

after tenth grade with the Experiment in International Living, and I spent all senior year in northern France with School Year Abroad. Travel provides a great opportunity to learn another language, live another culture, and see your own home with a new perspective. And your friends will still be there when you return. In fact, they'll want to hear all about your trip. Ask your guidance counselor, language teacher, or librarian for information. Or contact the Experiment at (800) 345-2929 or eil@worldlearning.org about general programs, or School Year Abroad at (978) 725-6828 or www.sya.org about studying in France, Spain, or China.

Dear Carol,
I think I might be a lesbian. I try to act really cool and pretty around girls at my school. Lots of people use the word "gay" as an insult. That makes me feel really weird and different.

Lesbian?

Dear Lesbian?,
Lots of girls try to act cool around girls just as lots of guys try to act cool around guys. That doesn't mean anybody is or isn't gay. Being gay means you're sexually attracted to someone of your own sex—meaning you'd rather, for instance, kiss or touch another girl than a boy. (At your age, some kids don't want to think about kissing or touching anybody yet and that's 100

percent normal, too!) There is no rush to label yourself, but if someday you realize that you are indeed more physically drawn to girls than guys, then thank your stars that you're living in this millennium. Because even though some ignorant kids use the word *gay* as an insult, many other kids and adults understand, accept, and appreciate all the ways people are different.

Dear Carol,
This is short but hard. I have secrets. Some of them no one knows. Not even my best friends. Are secrets better to keep to yourself? Or should I tell them? These secrets are not bad things I have done.

Secrets

Dear Secrets,
Are they bad things someone else has done that are now haunting you? If so, it might be good to talk to a trusted grown-up (parent, teacher, doctor, member of the clergy). But if your secret is something that is private but is not bothering you a lot (e.g. you have a crush, or you pick your split ends, or you sleep with six teddy bears), then it's fine to keep it to yourself. Use your judgment. And be aware that if anybody who makes you feel uncomfortable says, "This is our secret—don't tell your parents," your best move is probably to tell your parents.

Dear Carol,
I cry a lot. Happy times, sad times, scary times, when-
ever! People say to keep it in, but it's so hard! Is my
problem low self-esteem or am I too sensitive or is it
all just part of the unstoppable Mother Nature? Am
I normal?

Crybaby

Dear Crybaby,
As normal as I am. I've boohooed my way
through many a movie that has left the rest of my
family dry-eyed. Once when I was about five, my
big brother called me a crybaby in front of the
whole neighborhood—and it was so humiliating,
that I, well, cried! While it is better to express
your emotions than to bottle them up and better
to be sensitive than insensitive, do try to blink
back tears when you can. Are you getting enough
sleep or are you about to get your period? You're
more likely to weep if you're sleep-deprived or
premenstrual. Is something upsetting you? Little
things can also set you off if big things are bothering you. You may never be totally dry-eyed, but
I bet you will be able to hold back some of your
tears, and I encourage you to do things that will
make you feel strong and proud of yourself.

Dear Carol,
I have a big imagination. After school, I lock myself
in my room to dance. It's as if I'm in another world

and I'm a famous and beautiful princess. I can do this
for hours every day.

Oddball

Dear O.,
It's good to be imaginative and to enjoy solitude.
But if you're dancing for hours every day, you
aren't leaving yourself much time to be with others. Look into taking a dance class or art class or
getting involved with theater or an activity that
will keep you connected to others, too.

Feeling Depressed

Dear Carol,
A few years ago I was molested. I can't stop dwelling
on it. After I was molested, I felt like my soul was
taken away from me and I've found it very hard to
express my feelings. I have tried to tell two different
therapists about it, but I couldn't bring myself to talk
about it. I just kind of shut off to other people. I also
dress like a tomboy so I won't get molested again. It's
really hard to get a boyfriend when you look like a
boy. Can you give me some advice on how to forget
my pathetic history? It's messing up my life.

Messed Up

Dear Messed Up,
My heart goes out to you. I don't know what happened years ago, but it wasn't your fault, and

you've held it inside long enough. Just as you wrote to me, you can open up to a therapist. Does your school have a counselor? If not, or if you don't feel comfortable with him or her, get referrals from your doctor, a family friend, or member of the clergy, and have a quick talk on the phone with several therapists as you decide whom to talk to. Say, "Something happened to me and it's messing me up and I need to talk." See whose voice and manner you like best. Then set up an appointment and spill your story. If you can't say it out loud, write it down or draw a picture. You'll never forget your past, but you will be able to move forward. Other girls have had terrible experiences and have pulled through and begun to trust people again. You will, too. In fact, as you begin to accept that your past is part of you but is behind you, you'll confide in a few people and you'll find that other girls with seemingly picture-perfect lives have secrets of their own.

By the way, dressing like a tomboy doesn't automatically ward off molesters any more than dressing like a femme fatale guarantees a boyfriend. What you wear makes an impression, but when someone is molested, it's the molester who is to blame, not the girl or her skirt.

Dear Carol,
Sometimes I feel depressed. Not like I-feel-sad-today depressed, but like I can't sleep or eat or act normal.

This doesn't happen all the time. Maybe one or two times a month. Don't tell me it's PMS because I know it's not. I tried to talk to my friend about it, but she thought I was a freak. Is there something wrong with me?

Depressed?

Dear Depressed?,
I don't think so, and I'm sorry your friend wasn't more compassionate. I think it's normal, not freaky, to have mood swings, especially during adolescence. If your blues don't coincide with your period, I won't tell you it's premenstrual syndrome. But what does set you off? Start noticing. Test days? Track meets? When a crush ignores you? When it rains for 48 hours? When you are short on sleep? Pinpointing what makes you feel worse can help you feel better. Can you ask your parents or a doctor about this? If anyone in your family has ever suffered from clinical depression, that's an extra reason to monitor your emotions.

Dear Carol,
I've been feeling depressed. I'm struggling in math class, my parents treat me as an outcast and my brother as the Great One, and I'm having trouble finding out who my real friends are. I get blamed a lot and I feel like I'm guilty until proven innocent. I guess this is the main reason I feel like I might be

the D word: I started out with lots of activities—swimming, tumbling, 4-H, ceramics, horseback riding—and gradually lost interest in every one. I'm thinking about running away, but nothing is final. I haven't discussed this with anyone.

The Great Depression

Dear T.G.D.,

Lots of girls feel misunderstood by family and friends, and dropping activities in and of itself isn't alarming because it's appropriate to figure out which fields most interest you rather than always dabbling in dozens. But what might help you? Telling your parents you feel overlooked? Confronting your brother? Getting tutored in math? Finding that one sport or activity that holds your interest? Planning something (a party? trip?) to look forward to? All of the above? Start with a small step. Even rearranging one shelf can help you begin to regain a sense of control over your life.

Running away would not help. It would add to your troubles. What would you eat? Where would you shower? Where would you sleep? Too many runaways end up as prostitutes with worse problems than they ever imagined. In a few short years, you can move away instead of run away. You can start fresh at a college campus or with a job and roommate.

Does your school have a guidance counselor? Counseling *would* help! So would confiding in a favorite relative or teacher. Or having a heart-to-heart with your mom or dad, or even the supportive people who answer the Covenant House crisis line at (800) 999-9999. In serious cases, medications can also help. Hang in there. You will find your momentum again.

Dear Carol,

I feel like I'm on a cliff and I'm being pushed to the edge. I'm 13 and I find it hard to enjoy being a teenager. Really. My parents are divorced. My grades are bad. I have no real friends. And I feel as though my world is falling apart. I also cry a lot—what's up with that? Sometimes I lose sleep and go for days without eating. I feel like sometimes I want to die and be free of the world. I know you may think I'm stupid and crazy. I have a counselor, but I don't really want to tell her what's going on.

M.

Dear M.,

I don't think you are stupid and crazy. I think you are having a tough time, and it's hard to turn things around when you are feeling lower than lousy. Since you have a counselor, can you try harder to open up to her? (Or find a different counselor?) Believe me, counselors have heard it before—they spend their days listening to people in pain. They won't think, "She's nuts—what a whiner!" They'll think, "How can I help?" and then will help. Just talking it out helps. Can you try to talk to a parent or teacher?

You mention getting free of this world, but suicide is a permanent solution to temporary problems, and you want to change your life, not end your life. You want to find your place in the world, not free yourself of it. How? Can you pull up your grades in at least one course? Can you introduce yourself and confide in and listen to one new person, possibly someone whose parents are also divorced? Can you join one after-school group? Can you promise yourself (and me) that you won't skip meals but will take care of yourself? A few months (or weeks or days) or even one measly unexpected smile really can make a difference. You are more resilient than you think.

Dear Carol,
Hi. You probably don't remember me, but I sent you a letter and you wrote back. I wrote you and told you some of my problems. Well, I can say that my life is way better, good grades, good friends. I feel like I'm on top of the world. Thank you so much!
Later,

M.

Dear M.,
I sure do remember you, and I'm so glad to hear that you are feeling good again. Thanks for sharing

the news. Take care of yourself and if ever you do slip into another slump, you now know that you *can* turn things around—that spring does follow winter. Good luck and here's to you!

LET'S GET PHYSICAL
●●●●●

When I was in middle school, I wished I could have traded my braces for breasts, zapped my zits away, and been a natural athlete. How do you feel when you look in the mirror? How do you take care of your changing body? Do you get exercise on your own or on a team? Are you OK with having (or not having) your period? You may have lots of questions about body changes and body image. Me, I've got some answers.

Feeling Fuzzy

Dear Carol,
At what age should you begin to shave your legs?
Hairy

Dear Hairy,

There's no set age and if your hair doesn't bother you, don't bother it. The trouble with shaving is that once you start, you usually have to keep it up. Why? Because when hair grows back, it tends to come in stubby not silky. I'd wait as long as you can. Some women never shave their legs.

Dear Carol,

I think I need to shave. My friends made fun of me, and one boy said my leg hairs are longer than his. The problem is I don't know how to say anything to my mom without feeling uncomfortable. She's the type that turns BRIGHT red whenever I bring anything up. I'm already 13.

Chicken

Dear Chicken,

Feeling uncomfortable never killed anybody. Tell your mom why you've been thinking about shaving. Some moms are reluctant to recognize that their kids are growing up. Others just need a nudge now and then. Still others push their kids to grow up too fast. Instead of asking for your mom's permission to shave, you could ask what type of razor she recommends and whether she prefers to shave in the tub or sink. Instead of shaving, you could rub hairs off with a mitten product made of a superfine sandpaper. (Sounds bizarre, but you can find it in most pharmacies.) You could also bypass your mom and talk to an older sister or cousin or friend's older sister or mother. As for rude friends, can you tell them to knock it off? And notice which friends don't act mean—those are the keepers.

Dear Carol,
My friend doesn't shave her legs. All the kids make fun of her behind her back. I want to tell her to shave, but I'm afraid I'll hurt her feelings or she'll get mad at me.
                                                    Can't Break It To Her

Dear C.B.I.T.H.,
Maybe your friend is not in a mad rush to grow up and is resisting the pressures others feel. Can you stand up to the other kids? Say, "C'mon, give her a break," or "Who cares about her hairs?" or "I like her—could you please not make fun of her?" It may take guts, but it feels good to defend a friend. And why should she conform to other people's standards? If however, you do decide to draw her attention to her legs, you could walk through a pharmacy with your friend as you casually buy what you need, including razors, or you could even invite her to join you and a few friends for a Saturday spa—you'll provide the nail polish, razors, and shaving cream.

Dear Carol,
I have dark hair and love it—but not on my arms! I know everyone has arm hair, but mine is so dark.

One boy calls me "Monkey" and "Gorilla." It is very humiliating!

Gorilla

Dear G.,
If that particular imbecile were less cruel, would you feel differently? My guess is that no one besides you and him has given much thought to your arm hair. Attractive women come in all shapes, colors, sizes, and degrees of hairiness, and there's a lot to be said for learning to like your looks instead of struggling to change them. Then again, there's also a whole industry of hair-altering products and procedures that you can look into. Consult your mom or a trusted adult and try not to let that inane boy undermine your confidence. Let his immaturity be his problem, not yours!

Dear Carol,
I have dark facial hair between my nose and mouth. My baby-sitter told me I could dye it. Instead I shaved it and it stayed away for a while but then grew back. My godmother told me that was a bad idea. I want to buy removal cream, but my mom wants to check with my doctor first. Help! I feel ugly!

Hairy Situation

Dear H.S.,
Everyone has facial hair, and yours may not be as noticeable as you think, but I'm glad you're

able to talk openly with your mom and others. Pharmacies have shelves of bleaches (to lighten hair), depilatories (to dissolve it), and prewaxed strips (to remove it). Tweezing is also an option, and some women go to salons for the more long-lasting, painful, and expensive techniques of waxing, laser light, or electrolysis. Shaving is not ideal because shaved hair grows back quickly and dark stubble isn't the improvement you're hoping for.

Dear Carol,
Are you supposed to shave pubic hair? If you didn't, would it grow and grow and grow? Also I'm getting hair not just in my pubic area, but way above it! All the way to my belly button! Is that normal? My breasts are developing, my hips are widening, and I have hair ... but I don't have my period. I would pay money for my period! Write back—I don't want to ask anyone else about this.
                                                    Worried

Dear Worried,
You are not supposed to shave pubic hair, and it won't grow and grow and grow. You don't shave your eyebrows, right? And they know when enough is enough. A little hair beneath your belly button is fine, too, as is underarm hair. Hair, breasts . . . your period is next. But since you can't rush Mama Nature, you might as well enjoy these last years or months of girlhood and

of not having to fool with pads and tampons. Easier said than done, I know, because I was a late bloomer myself—I didn't get my period until I was 15 1/2!

Dear Carol,
I feel kind of embarrassed writing this but I guess I have to know. My pubic hair is fairly long but it's not curly. In school they said it would be curly.

Huh?

Dear Huh?,
Hair comes in different colors and textures and thickness whether it's on your head or in your undies.

Dear Carol,
I'm embarrassed to wear a bathing suit because I have a lot of hair by my bikini line. I tried shaving, but it grows back quickly and I get bumps, redness, and irritation, and it hurts. It would be a waste of time to bleach it every few weeks. I don't want to wear shorts for the rest of my life! My friends are not going through puberty as fast as I am, so they would laugh or not know what to say if I tried talking to them. I used to love summer but now I can't wait until winter.

Totally Needs Help

Dear T.N.H.,
Don't give up on summer! When it comes to puberty, it is hard to be ahead of or behind other

girls, but, in a few years everyone will be relatively caught up—and a lot less self-conscious. Meantime, you have options. You can decide: "Big deal. So I have a few extra dark and curlies." Or you can snip the hairs not covered by your bathing suit. Or you can bleach every few weeks—it's not that time-consuming. Or you can wax, which hurts for a moment but leaves you smoother longer; waxing two or three times during the bikini months would do the trick. Can you ask your mom about this? She may have had the same worries at your age.

Dear Carol,
Many girls write to your column saying they're embarrassed because they haven't started developing. Well, my problem is the opposite. NONE of my friends has any pubic hair AT ALL. (I know 'cause I'm on swim team.) I have a lot. When I change in the locker room I turn my back to them because I think they'll laugh or say I'm weird or something. Am I normal?
                                                              Confused

Dear Confused,
You're normal. Locker rooms bring out the insecurities in everyone and lots of girls turn wallward and dress like lightning. (I just made up the word *wallward*. I kind of like it, but don't use it in your next book report, OK?) Here's the thing: In a few years, your teammates will all have hit puberty and will be young women, not girls.

Some will be short, some tall, some big, some small, but everybody will be more physically developed and will have hair in all the expected places. For now, be patient and repeat after me: "I'm normal. I'm normal. I'm normal."

Too Short, Too Tall

Dear Carol,
I hate being short! At Six Flags, I can only go on the kiddie rides. Sometimes people who don't know me ask, "How old are you? Nine?" My friends are all tall, and I wish I would have a growth spurt!

Shrimp

Dear Shrimp,
You will. But for now there is nothing you can do about your height except accept it. Keep eating healthful foods and getting enough sleep, and before you know it, your favorite jeans will be flood pants. Of course, you may always be on the petite side, and that wouldn't be so terrible. I'm short, and the only drawback is that at movies I have to be careful never to sit behind ladies with big hair. Pluses? Since I don't look intimidating, nice people, short and tall, guys and girls, tend to feel comfortable around me right away. Yes, I could wear heels all day—just as tall girls could slump—but why invite backaches when it's easier to be who you are?

Dear Carol,
I am too tall and I look older than I am. Sometimes girls call me "Giant" or "Toothpick" and guys act scared of me even though I sometimes feel scared of them.
                                                    Too Tall

Dear Too Tall,
Your male and female classmates will eventually grow and grow up, and you won't feel so alone up there. Meantime, try to make peace with your changing body. You're not too tall—you're simply taller than your friends—and some of them probably envy you. Just as there are advantages and disadvantages to being short, there are pros and cons to being tall. Among the pros: You can look powerful on the job; you may have an edge in basketball and volleyball or modeling; and you may not have to worry about weight gain as much as shorter girls. For now, stand tall, and when you look in the mirror, give yourself a thumbs-up. (Go ahead, no one will know!)

Too Big, Too Small

Dear Carol,
All my friends are starting to wear bras. Well, that's because they have breasts. I wish I had breasts so much! I am a seventh-grader trapped in a third-grader's body and I feel really left out. I want to grow on top! The boys say I should get surgery. Should I?
                                                    Pancake

Dear Pancake,
No way! And fortunately no responsible doctor would put a healthy girl under the knife. I know it's hard to be patient, but you are still growing and though you may never be buxom, you will develop! Your breasts will appear and your self-consciousness will disappear. Besides, the point isn't to be pointy, it's to be fit and confident.

Dear Carol,
In gym class we have to change our clothes. All my friends' breasts are developing faster than mine. I'm kind of jealous. It's not like I look at their chests or anything, but I just notice. I wear a bra, but I'm flat as the floor. Is it OK to be jealous?
Jealous

Dear Jealous,
Sure. You're entitled to your feelings. But try not to obsess about breast size. I guarantee your breasts will grow, but you can't wish yourself into a B or C cup. In the big picture, attitude matters more than silhouette. Lucky girls aren't the ones who are flat or busty; lucky girls are the ones who accept themselves. (Did I know this when I was 13? No. But it was a great day when I finally realized that I'd never reach 5'3" or fill an A cup, and—so what!—I could still have a life.) Big is beautiful, medium is marvelous, and flat is fine. Really.

Dear Carol,
Before school each day, I started putting just a little
bit more tissue in my bra. When it looked like I was
truly developed, some tissues started coming out and
now everyone knows I stuffed. Today a boy said, "I
have a cold, do you have a Kleenex?" and some girls
started laughing.

Embarrassed

Dear Embarrassed,
Yipes, that is embarrassing! But guess what?
Your classmates made fun of you because they
feel as insecure as you do. Will they mature
emotionally? Yes. Will you mature physically?
Yes. Will the waiting period be hard for everybody? Yes. It's difficult, but try not to pay attention to the teasing because if you fume or cry
or call names, the jerky kids will know they
succeeded in getting you upset. Hold your
head high and work on accepting the body you
have.

Dear Carol,
My chest is bigger than the other kids'. I used to tape
them down, and now I exercise to make them go
away, but they won't. It is really embarrassing at
sleepovers when we change into our PJs. Some kids
say, "You are so lucky," but I don't feel lucky.

Growing Pains

Dear Growing Pains,
The growing years can be painful! Exercise won't make your chest shrink (any more than it made mine grow), but time is on your side, and you will soon feel less alone. For now, try to notice what you have in common with your friends (a love of pretzel goldfish or *Simpsons* reruns?) instead of focusing on physical differences.

Dear Carol,
Will I ever stop growing? Some of my friends have nothing on top, but I keep bursting out of my bras. One of my friends is always bugging me and saying, "You bra is showing," or "You should wear a higher-necked top."

Developed And Abnormal

Dear D. And A.,
You will stop growing and you are normal. But you may always be more voluptuous than your peers. The girl who teases you is probably uncomfortable with her own body and may envy yours. In junior high, lots of girls feel out of step. I get tons of letters from early bloomers *and* late bloomers. The good news is that most girls will soon stop worrying about breast size—theirs or yours.

Dear Carol,
My breasts are two completely different sizes! To make matters worse, I'm not that flat on either side.

I feel like an outsider. I see boys looking at my breasts all the time like I'm some sort of science project.
Freak Of Nature

Dear F. Of N.,
First of all, you are more aware of your body's asymmetry than anybody else. Second, a lot of junior-high boys spend a lot of time staring at a lot of girls' breasts. Third, you are still developing and chances are excellent that your breasts will even out. While you're not the only girl with uneven breasts, why not ask your doctor about this at your next checkup?

Dear Carol,
The skin on my breasts is transparent and there are purple-blue dots on them. Should I worry?
Worrying

Dear Worrying,
Nah. You can see purple-blue veins and dots on your wrists, too, right? But don't be embarrassed to ask the school nurse or a doctor your question. You may not even need to bare your entire breast.

Dear Carol,
One of my best friends is, well, I guess you could call her flat. It makes it hard to talk about things like what girls are going through. If she sleeps over, she's afraid of changing in front of me. If we're at the mall

and walk past an underwear store, she'll make jokes about bras or something. We can never really talk about girl things.

Growing Fast

Dear Growing Fast,
Just because your friend doesn't have a chest doesn't mean she doesn't have a brain—or feelings. Instead of giving up on your friend, include her. Talk about whatever is on your mind. She may feel left out at times, but that beats leaving her out on purpose, don't you think?

Dear Carol,
My best friend is kind of on the heavy side and we like to talk about girl things but whenever we do, she tries to compare our busts and says, "Mine are bigger than yours." It hurts to explain that it is just her heaviness that makes her chest big. I know I am right because I have noticed that the heavier she gets the more her bust grows. It's not that I'm jealous because I really don't care about my bust.

Starting To Get To Me

Dear S.T.G.T.M.,
The comparing sounds like a no-win proposition. Next time say, "It's not a contest." She may always be both bigger and more buxom than you—and that doesn't make either of you superior or inferior.

Dear Carol,
I'm seriously starting to develop, and in gym, my chest jiggles and sometimes hurts and everyone in my class wears at least a training bra or a sports bra. I don't. And I just can't scrape up the nerve to talk to my mom.

Embarrassed

Dear Embarrassed,
No one ever died of embarrassment, so it might be worth it to approach your mom even if you do redden and stammer. You could also write her a note. Or speak with another adult—an aunt? grandmom? Try, "I feel kind of awkward saying this, but could we shop for bras on Saturday?" Or ask your mom if she remembers talking to her mom about puberty. I remember wanting to wear a bra but not wanting to discuss it with my mom. A busty friend sensed my plight and handed me a care package—her hand-me-down training bras. I wore them proudly (thanks again, Anne) and weeks later, guess who suggested we go shopping? My mom!

Dear Carol,
It seems that some of the readers of your column are having trouble asking their parents for a bra. What worked for me was simply writing a note to my mother before I went to sleep. It said why I wanted (or needed) a bra, how I felt, and how I hoped she'd understand. I snuck it in her purse before she went to

work. Not only did I not have to say the word bra out loud, but it impressed my mother to know that I trusted her enough to tell her what was on my mind. Hope this helps another shy girl!

A Little Birdie

Dear A.L.B.,
Thanks. I bet it will.

Dear Carol,
My mom says I need to wear a bra to school, but I think they're dumb and uncomfortable.

Mad

Dear Mad,
For girls who jiggle in gym, bras aren't dumb; they're practical, and they lend support. As for comfort, some bras are more comfy than others. Go shopping and try on different styles. If you're feeling self-conscious, look for skin-color bras and for colorful tops that aren't revealing or see-through. If you don't think you need a bra yet, talk to your mom about which shirts look OK without one. Or ask her to buy you a tank or spandex top to wear beneath your shirt.

Dear Carol,
I have wanted a sports bra and finally the other day, I got two. But now the tight feeling around my chest makes me feel funny. Every time I raise my arms, the bra moves up, so I have to snap it back down again.

Do you think everyone notices that I have a bra? Also, should I act different now, you know, more mature?

Tight Bra

Dear T.B.,

Just as you aren't aware of when every single classmate wears a bra or has a pimple or gets new shoes or gains three pounds, the girls and guys in your class are more concerned with how they look than how you look. As for tightness, bras do take a little getting used to. Next time you go shopping, try on different styles and sizes until you find a bra that feels comfortable. Should you act more mature? Only if you want to. Just be you. Or as the Beatles sang: Obladi Oblada life goes on, bra!

Dear Carol,

I can't wear sleeveless tops because everyone will make fun of me because I don't wear a bra. If I do wear a bra, everyone will make fun of me because I don't need one. I doubt I'll ever have anything "up there." My mom is the same way.

Flat For Life

Dear F.F.L.,

I was desperate desperate desperate to wear a bra. Then da da DA DA! I triumphantly started wearing them. Then, months later, I realized I didn't truly need to after all. I'd also noticed a few models and dancers flaunting their boy-ish bodies. So I buried my bras in a drawer and decided to accept my body and that was that. Will you grow? Maybe. But if you really are flat for life, resolve to enjoy your sleek physique and to wear what you feel like wearing. Talk to your mom and take extra pride in whatever you like best about your body and in the fact that your body walks, runs, dances, and does what it is designed to do.

Dear Carol,
I'm not big-chested but I'm not flat either. Three kids in my class, including the boy I have a crush on, keep making a calculator say "Boobless" by writing 55319009 and then turning it upside down and stick-ing it in my face. It really hurts, especially when the boy I have a crush on does it.
Not Flat

Dear N.F.,
What total jerks! All I can say is life gets easier after middle school because even immature dorks usually figure out how to boost themselves up without putting others down. Meantime I have one question for you. Is your crush worthy of your devotion?

Dear Carol,
Boys try to feel my chest and shoot rubber bands at me. I told them to stop, but they wouldn't listen. I

didn't tell anyone because I was too scared. I didn't ask for this attention.

I Wish It Would Stop

Dear I.W.I.W.S.

Ugghh! They are so out of line! Talk to your parents, teachers, or principal. And if possible, with verve in your voice, tell those boys to back off. While some girls mature before others, most girls mature before boys. Don't let them stop you from feeling good about yourself.

When Will I Start? and Other Period Puzzles

Dear Carol,
I just went to get a physical, and the doctor said I was fine. She also said that I am going to get my period soon. I am 12 and I am scared.

Scared Of Puberty

Dear Scared Of Puberty,
You'd be even more scared if you started bleeding and you *hadn't* learned about menstruation. Nowadays, most American girls start around age twelve, though lots of girls start later, lots earlier. In your great-grandmother's day, the average age was around 14. You're smart to be looking ahead, but there's no need to be scared. Every woman you've ever met made it through her first period.

When you do start, you won't suddenly be gushing down there. You'll lose just six or so tablespoons of blood over the course of several days. Don't worry—your body makes more. You'll use pads or tampons, changing them every few hours or as needed, and you may have cramps. Since you may also feel extra tired, try to go to bed early and eat extra healthfully.

Worried about starting at school or at camp or away from home? Buy some pads now. With handy pads hidden in a plastic bag in your backpack or locker, you'll feel less anxious. Worried a tampon could somehow get lost inside you and go floating around your body? Relax. Can't happen.

Dear Carol,
I haven't had my period but I have had some milky whitish yellowish discharge so I think I'll get it soon. I have been using tampons to get used to them. Will this hurt me to use them before I have my period?
                                                    Concerned

Dear Concerned,
Do NOT use tampons when you are not having your period because they could chafe or irritate your vagina. Use a pad or liner if you think you might start on any given day, but do not put absorbent materials in your vagina at a time

when there's not much to absorb. This is one case when practicing ahead of time is not a good idea.

Dear Carol,
I know that if you occasionally have yellow or clear liquid in your panties from you-know-where, then your period is on its way. This has been happening to me for years, but I haven't gotten my period yet. Not that I want my period or anything, but I'd like to know when my period should come.

Wondering

Dear Wondering,
In this high-tech world, there are still a few mysteries. When an individual girl will start is one of them. Skinny girls tend to start later; heavier girls and African-American girls tend to start earlier. The discharge you describe is normal, but there's no formula for pinpointing when you'll start. Sorry about that!

Dear Carol,
How come some days you get a heavy flow and some days you get a light flow? I don't get it.

Without A Clue

Dear Without,
Once you hit puberty, you are capable of becoming a mother and your body gets prepared every

month for the possibility of taking care of a fertilized egg. Assuming you have not had unprotected sex, there is no way a sperm could have hooked up with one of your eggs, so you definitely cannot be pregnant. Once your body catches on that it doesn't need the velvety lining that has been building up inside your uterus, it discards the lining, disintegrated egg, and some body fluids. That's your period: a few days' worth of reddish brown stuff that usually flows lightly then heavily then lightly again.

If you mark a little x on your calendar on the first day of your period, you will be able to anticipate when your next period will come. When your periods become regular, you'll know whether your cycle is 28 days or more or less, and you won't be caught totally by surprise the next month. You can even keep several products handy: liners, thin pads, or slim or junior tampons for lighter days; thick pads or regular or super tampons for heavier days. During the heaviest times, you can wear a tampon and put a pad in your underwear. (But don't put on your new white undies.)

Dear Carol,
I started my period three to four months ago and haven't had it since. Did I really start or was it a false alarm? I'm freaked!

Girly Problems

Dear G.P.,
Welcome to womanhood. Yes, you probably really started. Most women have regular periods every month, but many girls have periods that are irregular. As long as you are a virgin, there's no way you can be pregnant, so don't worry about that. Your changing body is just sorting itself out. Hmm, if you are quite young, let me add that it is possible that you did not start yet, but that the blood you saw actually came from your hymen. The hymen is a little bit of skin inside the vagina. It can get torn during sports, and that can cause spotting that has nothing to do with menstruation. Not to worry though—this would still be no reason to freak!

Dear Carol,
I just got my period and I have tons of tampon questions for beginners. What brand should I use? What size? With or without applicators? (Blush!!!!) Where do you insert one? And what about TSS?

Worried

Dear Worried,
There are many good name-brand and generic products. As for size, if you're a small girl with a light flow, slim or junior should do the trick. If you have a heavier flow, try regular or super. It's best to use the lowest absorbency required. You can use supers on heavy days, regular tampons on lighter days. Many products include applicators

and many don't and it makes no difference. Some girls find plastic applicators with rounded tips easiest to use, but they aren't biodegradable and should never be flushed down toilets. Where to insert the tampon? Into your vagina! Aim toward the small of your back and push it in just far enough so that you don't really even feel it. There's an illustrated instruction sheet in the box, and if you take your time, you'll be able to figure it out. Don't let the tiny print about toxic shock syndrome scare you because after an outbreak in 1980 (forever ago!), that disease has become very, very rare. It's still a good idea to change tampons not just when necessary, but at least every six to eight hours. The best way to tell if it's time for a change is to tug gently on the string. If the tampon stays put, it's not time yet. When it is time, it will slide out easily. If you go to sleep wearing a tampon, do change it in the morning. And if, God forbid, you ever do experience the symptoms of TSS—high fever, vomiting, dizziness, diarrhea—when wearing a tampon, yank it out and call your doctor.

Dear Carol,
In school this year we take showers after gym. I don't feel comfortable with this because I have always kept to myself about my body and what if I have my period on gym day and my tampon string shows?
                                        Shower and Tampon Strings

Dear S.T.S.,
If your string shows, your string shows. If you were to start spying, you might notice other girls showering during their time of the month, too. Everybody's body is changing right now and many girls feel as uncomfortable as you do. To avoid the possibility of strings-in-the-shower, on a light day, you could go to the bathroom and remove your tampon before showering, then put in a fresh one afterward.

Dear Carol,
When my mom and aunt and sister have their peri-
ods, they don't go swimming. They say, "I just can't."
Why can't they?

Wondering

Dear Wondering,
A woman who uses pads cannot swim with them because the pads would become waterlogged and look bulky under a bathing suit, and because a wet pad would not be effective. If a woman uses tampons instead of pads, she can swim to her heart's content. Tampons are also ideal for gymnastics and other active sports.

Dear Carol,
How can I talk to my mom about girl stuff? It's so
awkward!

Embarrassed

Dear Embarrassed,
An awkward talk may be better than no talk at all. Say, "Mom, my body has really been changing," or "I'm embarrassed, but I have questions about puberty." Or write your questions in a note and ask her to write the answers back. Or e-mail them! If she's embarrassed, too, you can learn from books and brochures, relatives, friends, health teachers, sisters and mothers of friends, camp counselors, nurses, or doctors.

Dear Carol,
I started my period early, and my mom thinks it's a complete joke. She always goes around telling everyone about it. I've sat down to talk with her and I've asked her to please stop telling it to people. She always says, "OK, I won't," then goes off and tells more people. How can I stop her?
Mom Won't Stop

Dear M.W.S.,
If this book were for moms, I'd tell her for you. Instead I'm encouraging you to let her know once again that you'd like her to be discreet. Without shouting or whining, say, "Mom, it may be no big deal to you that I started, but it's a big deal to me, and I really wish you wouldn't tell anybody. If you want me to share personal stuff with you, I have to know you won't tell anyone." Can't bring yourself to say the words? Write a

note and put it on her pillow or in her purse. Or show her this chapter.

Dear Carol,
When I have my period, I don't like telling my mom. When we're out, she asks if I need to change my pad even when I just have to go to the rest room.
Private

Dear Private,
Most moms mean well, and it's not always easy for a mom to watch her little girl become a young woman. Still, enough is enough. Next time she makes a well-intentioned but unwelcome comment, say, "Mom, I know you're trying to be helpful, but I have all this under control." If you give her a smile instead of getting mad, that will help, too.

Dear Carol,
My parents are divorced and they have joint custody and I don't like to talk about personal things with my dad. I'm afraid I'm going to have my period at his house, and I don't think he'll know what to do.
Help Wanted

Dear H.W.,
You probably have jammies and a toothbrush at your dad's. Buy pads and liners at any pharmacy or supermarket and stash them at the back of a

-69-

drawer at his place, too. That way, if your dad doesn't know what to do, you will, and you'll be ready. If your last period started one month ago, and you're off to your dad's, put a liner in your underwear and extra supplies in your backpack. Worst case scenario: You waste a liner—and gain peace of mind. Still worried? You can always call your mom from your dad's. (P.S. It's also very possible that your dad will know what to do and even be cool about it.)

Dear Carol,
I'm 13 and I hate menstruating. I always get very depressed when I have my period. I have these awful crying fits and I feel totally miserable. I feel that having my period at such an early age is really un-necessary. I'm not planning to get married and have a baby anytime soon. So I'm asking you if there is any way to make it stop aside from starving myself which I have tried. Please don't give me a lecture about how having your period is a healthy, normal thing. I know that, but I don't care, I hate it, and I just want to know if there's a way to get rid of it.

Bloody Tired

Dear B.T.,
I'll spare you the lecture about the merits of menstruating because you're right, it is "unnec-essary" to start at such a tender age. That said, you can't turn back the clock on puberty. You can ask your mom or doctor about medications

to relieve discomfort. And you can welcome the news that your periods may get easier and you will get more used to them.

Starving yourself is NEVER a good idea. Some girls in times of famine or in concentration camps (or even in rigorous athletic training) do temporarily stop menstruating because Mother Nature doesn't think they'd be good bets for pregnancy and childbirth. But their periods don't permanently disappear, and in the case of gaunt and hungry women, their bodies are in distress.

To tell you the truth, that "time of the month" is not your average adult woman's personal favorite week either. But hey, let's be grateful that we live in a world with pads and tampons. Your great-grandmom didn't have it so easy. Before 1921, women wore cloth diapers that they washed and reused. After that they wore bulky napkins held up by a belt contraption. Finally in 1936 tampons were introduced.

One more thought. While I (and every other female) hate to feel upset and have some guy say, "Oh, you're just having your period," it is nonetheless helpful to be aware of whether you tend to be fragile or crotchety (CROTCHety? now that's an interesting word!) right on schedule each month. If you're losing it or wondering why *everyone* around you has an attitude problem, and it's rag-time, remind yourself, "My life doesn't stink—I just have my period." (P.S. Do not rush to share this insight with the male of the species. We're allowed to acknowledge the link between moodiness and menstruation. They aren't.)

Eating Well

Dear Carol,
I eat too much junk food and not enough health food. I love chocolate—and I hate veggies. The only veggie I do like is potatoes. I don't like many fruits either. I also hate breakfast food, so usually I have just a brownie or something. The weird thing is, I'm not one pound overweight. And you know how they say if you don't eat a healthy breakfast, you won't do well in school? Well, I've gotten straight A's since Day One. I still want to stop eating so much junk, but even the sight of veggies makes me want to hurl.

Chocoholic

Dear Chocoholic,
I congratulate you for being a good student and wanting to eat more healthfully. You don't have to give up chocolate and junk food, but yes, your body will thank you if you eat more nutritiously. You say you don't like breakfast food. How about frozen pizza or hot soup or even a baked potato instead of that brownie? You say you don't like many fruits. Which do you like? Make sure your

parents (or you) keep those fruits around. As for veggies, get yourself to tolerate salad or one colorful vegetable—cherry tomatoes, baby carrots, yellow peppers, or green broccoli. And try a new vegetable this week—maybe raw with a dip or cooked in a sauce.

Remember the food pyramid? Variety is important. Besides fruits and vegetables, your body needs bread, rice, cereal, or pasta (ideally whole-wheat) to fill you up and keep you going; meat, chicken, fish, eggs, or beans for protein; and milk, cheese, or yoghurt for calcium to build strong bones. Allergic to lactose? Drink lactose-free milk. You might also want to take vitamins, or eat fortified cereals or drink orange juice with calcium. The important thing is to take care of your body—it's the only one you've got!

Dear Carol,
I've been reading all these nutrition articles and they say stuff like "six servings a day of bread, cereal, or pasta" and "eight glasses of water a day." I don't know about everyone else, but I don't eat and drink that much every day! What is the real deal?
Nutrition

Dear Nutrition,
Some people eat more than others, and some need to because they are big or are always on the go or have fast metabolisms. The real deal is to

eat a variety of foods that are good for you and to drink as much water as you can. (Take a sip when you pass the water fountain.) As for the pyramid, an official serving is smaller than a typical serving, so six servings of grains may sound like a huge quantity, but one mere slice of bread actually counts as one full serving. You may be eating enough nutritious foods after all.

Dear Carol,
All my life I've eaten pork and beef. I want to stop. I can't stand to eat a poor animal that grew up not knowing that when it got big and fat, it would be killed and eaten. The problem is, my favorite foods are hot dogs and hamburgers. My mom says it's just part of life.

Carnivore

Dear Carnivore,
Welcome to the world in which things are never as simple as they seem. It is hard to think about the slaughter of animals, but becoming a vegetarian is not a snap decision. Why don't you cut back on your meat-eating and perhaps resolve not to eat veal since veal is made from baby cows that never get to grow up? You might consider buying free-range chicken since they get to run around (better for them, healthier for you) instead of spending their short lives in cages. And can you learn to love veggie burgers? Some people swear by them!

Dear Carol,
I really want to go vegetarian. I think it's mean to kill animals that deserve to live. I want to tell my parents, but they love meat.

Trying To Veggie Out

Dear Trying,
If you're thinking about cutting out meat, think about adding to your diet, too. A diet of macaroni, fries, and candy may be vegetarian, but it sure isn't healthful, and I don't want you to wind up anemic. Can you develop a taste for leafy vegetables, fresh fruits, and brown rice with lentils, peas, or beans? Can you snack on apricots, dates, almonds, raisins? Do you like peanut butter and jelly sandwiches? Would you enjoy concocting creative salads and soups? Do you like tofu? Can you make it a game to eat a variety of colorful foods? Will you take iron supplements? If you're going to consider becoming a vegetarian (or a vegan, who doesn't even eat fish or eggs or cheese), read up about it before approaching your parents. They will take you more seriously when they see that you are taking yourself more seriously. They may also be willing to order in or cook vegetarian food sometimes—especially if you help set the table or clean up.

Dear Carol,
I know this sounds weird, but I don't think I weigh enough. I'm so skinny! My legs are disgusting. I'm

embarrassed to wear shorts because of my stick legs.
Is there any way I can gain weight?

Miss Stick

Dear Miss Stick,
I get more letters from girls who feel too fat than girls who feel too thin, but you aren't alone. I was a bit of a stick myself until senior year when I was lucky enough to live in Brittany, France. I indulged in French bread, cheeses, and pastries, and . . . my metabolism caught up with me. Yours will, too. Here at home, you can help yourself to extra pizza or pasta, nuts and raisins, or, say, a banana milkshake. Don't sneak Snickers; try to eat healthfully. Your body may be using its energy right now to shoot upward, but soon you're sure to put on a little weight. If you exercise or go out for a sport, your legs will develop more muscles and your body will be better toned. Questions? Ask a school nurse or a doctor. And ask your parents if they were skinny at your age. If they still are, and you think you always will be, start embracing it—there are worse fates.

Dear Carol,
I'm fat. I see all these TV shows of how to get skinny and toned, but I can't get psyched. One commercial talked about a kind of candy bar that if you eat it you can lose weight. Sometimes I try to diet, but then I sneak food and I'm back to square one. Help!

Fat As A Pig

Dear F.A.A.P.,

Being slim isn't everything, but being fat is no fun and is not healthy. To turn things around, start by turning off the TV. There's no such thing as a magic diet candy bar, and while most lose-weight gimmicks and pills are nonsense, some are downright dangerous.

The best way to trim down is to eat less. At meals take smaller portions, eat slowly, put down your fork between bites, and try to wait ten minutes before jumping up for seconds—give your tummy a chance to feel full. Drink low-fat milk or water or nutritious juices, and skip the caloric sodas. Ask your parents to stock up on grapes, melon, carrots, celery sticks, and other fruits and vegetables instead of leaving junky snacks around. Chips and fries are full of fat. Switch to pretzels or unbuttered popcorn, but don't go overboard on them either. And don't keep food in your room—eat only in the kitchen. Desserts? Resist or share. (It's OK to have some M&M's, not to inhale a giant bag.) When you do say no to something you like, quietly give yourself a pat on the back. If you think it would help, write down what you eat for a few days. Between meals, brush your teeth, chew sugarless gum, or sip tea.

It's ideal to go out for an organized sport or enjoy one on your own, but any activity beats inactivity.

Like to garden? Get out and garden. Or hike or bike or dance. Or do sit-ups or stretches, maybe with a friend or a workout video. Walk instead of going by bus, car, or elevator. Keep moving. Help your body be fit and healthy.

If you can eat a little less and exercise a little more without counting every calorie or getting obsessive, I guarantee you will begin to look and feel better within two weeks. Your goal isn't to diet; it's to improve your habits. Slowly and sensibly you can lose weight—and gain confidence.

Dear Carol,
I'm very overweight, and I don't like it. I want to lose weight so much, I'm even considering becoming anorexic. Please write back on how to lose weight and please do not write something like "Weight does not matter; it's what's inside that counts." I hate when I get that answer.

Oink Oink

Dear O.O.,
I'm sorry you're feeling low and I'm glad you're motivated to do something about it. Weight does matter. If you are "very overweight," then it would be good for your health, confidence, and social life to lose a few pounds—sanely. Learn about calories (from books or magazines) and hold back on junk food, seconds, and refills. Say no to empty calories—and say yes to yourself!

Starvation is not a weight-loss plan, and anorexia is a scary disease. What's inside you matters, too, so don't lose sight of your many good qualities as you strive to get into shape.

Dear Carol,
My mom says I need to lose some weight. I don't really think I do because I'm thinner than the girls in the group I hang out with. But most of those girls are pretty big. I asked them if I was fat, and they said no. I don't want to hurt my mom's feelings, but how do I get her to lay off?

Annoyed

Dear Annoyed,
The point isn't to be thin; it's to be fit, healthy and confident. And some girls are naturally heavier than others. Why is your mom on your case? Is she trying to be annoying? Is she overly concerned with her own body? Or is she trying to be helpful whereas your friends are trying to be nice? Maybe your mom was overweight in school and didn't feel good about it. Maybe she realizes that girls and guys often judge each other in superficial ways, and she has your best interests at heart.

Consider telling your school nurse, health teacher, or doctor that you're not fishing for a compliment, you're seeking a professional opinion about your weight. And tell your mom not to pressure you. If you decide you do want to shape up a little, you may want to enlist her help so she can, for instance, stock up on fruit instead of fruit roll-ups. Next step: exercise and avoid these four S's: soda, sweets, seconds, snack foods.

Dear Carol,
I think society pressures girls to be thin. My dad told me tonight that I could lose a little weight, and it hurt me. I'm usually very happy with the way I am but when he said that, I was crushed. Is there a certain way you have to look or should you just look like you?

Confused

Dear Confused,
It is confusing! I think the ideal is to look your best as naturally and effortlessly as possible. In other words, bathe and wear clean clothes, but don't spend hours doing your hair or makeup. As for weight, your dad's comment hurt (ouch!) but was he trying to hurt you or help you? Was he off base or not? It's great that you're usually happy with the way you are—don't lose that winning attitude! And girls often gain a little weight before puberty. But it's possible, too, that your dad noticed that you were putting on pounds without realizing it (maybe because you're now spending more time at your desk than at the playground?). Listen to your body and eat at

meals and when you're hungry—not just when something yummy is within reach. At restaurants, share one dessert for the table instead of ordering your own. And junk the junk food.

By the way, you're right that society pushes thinness. Many models are clinically anorexic. You don't want to be underweight, especially during your growing years. But many teenagers are overweight, even obese, and that's not ideal either. If you need to, you can find the willpower to summon your won't power—without turning into a person who starts each day on a scale or who frets nonstop about weight. (Major brain drain.)

Dear Carol,
My friend always says I need to lose weight. I want to talk to her but I can't.
Can't Stand It

Dear C.S.I.,
Friends are supposed to build each other up, not tear each other down. You could try, "I'm fine with how I look and I wish you'd stop making comments. Worry about your looks if you want—not mine." You can also decide not to let her criticism bug you. As Eleanor Roosevelt put it, "No one can make you feel inferior without your consent."

Dear Carol,

I've been overweight and double-chinned for a long time and I've been trying to work it off, but in the meantime, I have to shop in the women's departments. I can't go shopping with friends because I'm too embarrassed.

Help!

Dear Help!,

There's no crime in being bigger (or smaller) than your friends. Instead of shopping together, why not go skating or walking or blading together? Or shop with a friend who is not judgmental or who also wears larger sizes.

Dear Carol,

I'm writing this in tears. I'm so fat! I hate myself. Why can't I lose weight? I've tried starvation and nothing—I lost, like, two pounds. I can't even be bulimic because I hate barfing. It sucks.

Chubby

Dear C.,

I'm sorry you're feeling miserable. Instead of hating yourself, take two minutes right now to think about what you love about yourself. In America, more people are overweight than underweight. And it is hard to lose inches and pounds. But think health and moderation, not starving and barfing! Your body needs fuel (food) every day for energy and to grow.

The best way to lose weight isn't to stop eating or start vomiting, (those methods make you sick); it's to eat less and exercise more.

People who starve themselves on purpose have a disease called anorexia. Some become rail thin but still think they're fat, and some become weak and almost skeletal and do permanent damage to their bodies. Some anorexics die.

People who throw up (or purge) after eating have an even more common eating disorder called bulimia. Maybe you know someone who thinks she's pulling a fast one because she'll eat a big sundae, then vomit and think, "Hurray! No calories." What she may not know is that she's messing up her body by causing chemical imbalances and dehydration. When stomach acids enter her mouth, they can also harm her teeth and gums.

Anorexics, bulimics, and binge eaters (people who gorge compulsively) often wind up feeling depressed and need professional help to learn how to eat healthfully again. Don't go off the deep end when it comes to eating. If something is bothering you, don't take it out on your body. Talk it out with a trusted friend, parent, relative, or counselor.

Dear Carol,
Every time I look in a mirror, I see a huge fat person. It sometimes makes me cry and sometimes makes me

want to starve myself. If I tell my parents, they'll make me quit gymnastics, which is where I probably get my ideas about being fat. My friends think anyone who would starve herself is a jerk, so I can't tell them. Is this all my fault? How can I stop comparing myself to other people? I feel like a blimp, but friends say I'm too thin. I weigh myself a lot and obsess about a pound. Sometimes my parents try to make me eat something, but I hide it or throw it away. When I do eat, I get really mad at myself. I also am afraid that if I gain any weight, I'll lose my coolness. At school we're learning about eating disorders, and I'm getting sort of scared.

Too Fat Or Too Thin?

Dear Too Fat Or Too Thin?,
Since you're scaring yourself, maybe you're ready to stop yourself from getting really sick. I'm glad you were brave enough to write me, and I encourage you to try to go three days eating meals without hiding or discarding food. If you can't, you need to get help to regain your health and to figure out what's "eating" you and why you are driven to starve yourself. Girls who starve themselves aren't jerks—they're people with a frightening eating disorder called anorexia which, in serious cases, can be fatal. Is it all your fault that you sometimes equate thinness with coolness and are tempted to deprive your body of the food it needs to stay alive? No. And

no, you shouldn't have to quit gymnastics. But do talk to an adult who can be there for you as you learn how to accept and care for yourself. Call the National Association of Anorexia and Associated Disorders (847) 831-3438; American Anorexia/Bulimia Association (212) 575-6200; or Eating Disorders Awareness and Prevention (206) 382-3587. Or check out this website: www.aabainc.org.

Dear Carol,
One of my friends thinks she's fat, which she definitely is not. She hasn't been eating for over two weeks. When she does eat, she'll have an orange, apple, or a piece of gum and that's it for the day. All her friends tell her to eat, but she refuses. One day during science, she looked the worst ever. She looked dead, and she was cold (on a hot day). She could barely hold in her tears. I don't think her mom knows—or maybe her mom is doing it, too. I don't know who to tell, and if she finds out I told a teacher or counselor, she might not speak to me.

Afraid

Dear Afraid,
What a heartbreaking letter. Your friend is lucky you care about her. You could tell a teacher or counselor or school nurse and ask that person not to use your name, and/or you could call her parents directly (at work?) and express your

concern. Your friend isn't just flirting with anorexia; she's in the danger zone—she is literally starving to death. You don't want her to be mad at you, but even more important, you don't want her to die. Find an adult to help you help her. You'd be speaking up not to betray her but to save her.

I know a 17-year-old whose three closest friends banded together and told her, "If you can't eat without throwing up or using laxatives for two days, we're going to your mom." The girl couldn't, so her friends talked to her mother, and the girl is now getting the help she desperately needed.

Dear Carol,
My best friend thinks she is fat, but she's average. The problem is she rarely eats lunch. It might be because her boyfriend sits at her table and his family thought she was fat. We tell her to eat, but she won't. She has recently lost about fifteen pounds, and we don't know what to do. We think she might have an eating disorder.

Concerned For Her Health

Dear C.F.H.H.,
There's a difference between having an eating disorder and having less-than-ideal eating habits. Your friend would be much better off having a small soup or salad rather than skipping lunch,

but that doesn't mean she's necessarily heading for trouble. In fact, if she lost fifteen pounds and is still about average in weight, she may deserve your support rather than criticism. It's hard to shed excess pounds, and she did it! If, however, she keeps on losing weight and skips other meals, too, you'd be right to share your worries with an adult.

Dear Carol,
I was looking through some old Girls' Life magazines and some girls think they're anorexic but I don't think they are. In fact I'm almost positive. My sister has anorexia and she had to go to a hospital because she was so skinny that she was dying. I know what anorexia looks like, and there is a big difference between not eating your lunch and not eating for seven days straight. Anorexia is a serious and deadly disease that takes lives. It's no joke. I've seen my own sister dying and to sum it up, it's not funny or cool to have your fingers turn blue.
A Person Who Knows

Dear A.P.W.K.,
Thank you for writing. I hope your sister gets better and stays better.

Dear Carol,
My best friend and I are overweight. Since last year, we've been starving ourselves and making ourselves

throw up when we do eat. At the beginning of last month, I started throwing up blood with my food also. Then my friend signed up for modeling and in the class, she realized that everyone else was very skinny. So we got even more serious about starving ourselves and making ourselves throw up and now my best friend is thinking of suicide because she can't take it anymore. What should I do? I know I'm supposed to tell an adult that I trust, but I can't because we'll both get in trouble. I want to tell my mom, but I'm too embarrassed and ashamed of what we've been doing.

Needing Help To Hold On To Life

Dear N.H.T.H.O.T.L.,
Tell your mom. You're both already in trouble—you're vomiting blood and your best friend is suicidal! Why wait until you're in the hospital and she's dead? If you just can't tell your mom, tell your dad or aunt or grandmother or school counselor or someone who can see that you two don't need scolding or grounding, you need professional help—you need to be rescued and taught how to believe in and take care of yourselves. Don't wait another minute to talk with a responsible adult. Please let the very next meal you eat stay in your stomach. And the one after that.

Skin Care

Dear Carol,
Help! I've been getting pimples on my nose and chin and I hate it! I'm afraid I'm going to crack the mirror.
Mountain Range

Dear Mountain Range,
Look away from the mirror, and around school. You're not the only one with an unwanted blemish or two—or ten. If you feel truly polka-dotted, consult a dermatologist. (Worked for me.) Meantime wash your face gently at least twice a day, eat healthful food, get enough sleep and exercise, drink lots of water, keep your hands and hair off your face, and consider using cover-up makeup or zit products. Tempted to squeeze a big mama pimple? Don't. Leave it alone. If you can't resist, wet a washcloth with really hot water and place it against your pimple for a good couple of minutes. Apply slight pressure, and the mini volcano may erupt on its own. Finally, rinse your face with warm then cold water. Pimpling outside means maturing inside. Be patient. This too shall pass.

Dear Carol,
My mom and I get in big fights every summer because she is paranoid about skin cancer and is constantly trying to smear sunscreen all over me. I'm surprised

she doesn't make me wear a winter coat to the beach.
Enough Already

Dear E.A.,
A shawl on the shore might be a bit much, but a layer of sunscreen makes good sense. Ever since my husband got a melanoma (yes, skin cancer) on his knee and had to have surgery to get rid of it, he and I have taken the news about skin cancer a lot more seriously. His dermatologist says a burn is evidence of sun damage. He also says to use a sunscreen that has an SPF factor of at least 15 and that blocks out UVA and UVB light. That way you are protecting yourself from skin cancer and your skin will look smoother longer. Since you're tired of running from your mom, take responsibility for your own health and apply a sunscreen before you hit the beach and later again at the beach. And while your winter coat belongs in the closet, how about a summer hat? Try on several and buy the one that looks most fetching. (If you're desperate for a tan, go for a fake-bake by using a tanning cream. Follow directions, though, or you could end up orange.)

Dear Carol,
I have this wart on my hand and I'm afraid that if boys or my friends see it, they won't like me. Some people have seen it and asked what it was. I said a scab. I really want to get rid of it. It is ruining my life!
Wartie

Dear W.,

Don't let a little wart ruin your big life. And don't imagine that people would write you off if they only knew. If you become quiet and withdrawn, people may keep their distance, but if you're friendly, you'll have friends. As for the wart, you could consult a dermatologist or ask a pharmacist or doctor about over-the-counter medications. But warts are weird and often come and go all by themselves. You can have a wart removed, then notice that it has grown back. Or you can ignore a wart completely then notice that it has—hurray!—disappeared on its own.

Me and My Big Mouth

Dear Carol,
I have big teeth and it makes me feel ugly and stupid.
My mother says I'm beautiful the way I am, but I
don't think so.

Ugly Duckling

Dear U.D.,

Many girls feel self-conscious about something— teeth, feet, ears, breasts—and one of the great things about getting older is that you make peace with your body. (Scratch that. On second thought, lots of older people never quite accept their bodies and go to bizarre lengths to look younger again!)

While dentists can help with stained, broken, crooked, or pointy teeth, they can't do much about size. Which means that you might as well come to terms with having a million-dollar smile. Do you judge people mostly by the size of their bodies or features? Or by how caring and fun and smart they are? Focus on what you like about yourself, and remember what happened to the ugly duckling. Even in real life, there are happy endings.

Dear Carol,
I am ashamed to smile at people. See, I used to drink Coke and coffee and eat a lot of candy and I didn't brush my teeth that much. Now my teeth are stained and have a yellow coating. Any suggestions?
Ashamed To Smile

Dear Ashamed To Smile,
See your dentist about cleaning and bleaching. Then keep brushing (whether your mom reminds you or not), and smile! I guarantee your classmates don't all have shiny white teeth—many probably have shiny colorful braces. Besides, your smile is more important than your teeth. Whom would you rather hang out with? A girl with perfect pearlies or a girl who acts friendly?

Dear Carol,
I'm afraid to put my face near other people's (especially boys') faces because I'm afraid I have bad

breath. I'm especially worried when I'm slow dancing with a boy.

Bad Breath

Dear B.B.,
More people worry about bad breath than have it. If you brush your teeth (and even tongue) with toothpaste morning and night, and avoid garlic and onions before dates or dances, you should be ahead of the game. Ask your mom or sibling if you need to use mouthwash or breath mints. Then talk, smile, laugh, and slow dance! Commercials and ads get people worrying about all sorts of nonproblems so that we'll race off to buy expensive products. If you really have reason to believe you have halitosis (chronic bad breath), visit your dentist or doctor, and keep gum or mints handy.

Odor Issues

Dear Carol,
I think I need deodorant but my mom hasn't mentioned it and I'm too nervous to say anything. I wish she would treat me like a preteen!

Preteen Jitters

Dear Preteen Jitters,
Maybe she's waiting for you to mention it. Or maybe you don't need deodorant—not everyone

sweats much, and if you take frequent showers or baths, you probably smell fine. You can say in person or in a note, "Mom, I've been thinking about using a deodorant. Any suggestions?" They come in various brands, strengths, and forms. Next time you're at a pharmacy, take a look.

Dear Carol,
I am 13 and I have a problem with my body that I don't want to ask anybody else about. I think it's something that I can control, but I am clueless on how. My armpits sweat so much even though I wear deodorant and shave. Is it just me? I need to know how to stop it and soon! Today at school I wore a tight orange shirt and I got big wet spots under my arms. It happens every day! It's not because of heat because I sweat when it is cold. Help!
Big Wet Spots

Dear B.W.S.,
You can't control how much you sweat, and shaving does not affect sweating. While you're waiting for your hormones to settle down, keep taking morning showers, and wear clean cotton or well-ventilated clothes (dampness shows less when shirts are loose and dark or patterned) or wear a light absorbent undershirt so telltale spots won't show. Antiperspirants fight perspiration whereas deodorants fight odor, and you can find a product that does both. You can also discuss this with your doctor.

Dear Carol,
One of our friends has body odor. We don't know
how to tell her, but we need to for the sake of the
school. The boys are making fun of her, too, and I
don't think she realizes she has a problem.

Needs A Gas Mask

Dear N.A.G.M.,
Hygiene is a touchy subject so please don't gang
up on your friend and chant "P.U. B.O.!" But
if you and she are alone, you can say in a no-
big-deal way, "Look, I feel awkward saying this,
but I think you might want to use a deodorant.
I use one." Or after gym, ask if she wants to borrow yours. Your other alternatives are to ask a
health teacher to tell her, put an anonymous (but
gentle) note in her locker, keep mum, or say
something like, "Some older kid just sat by me
in study hall and you could tell she forgot to
use deodorant." Or go in a drugstore together
and when you pass the deodorants, pretend you
are looking for one and have her help you pick
it out.

Dear Carol,
I have a friend whose breath stinks. I try not to cover
my nose but it smells like she woke up and did not
brush her teeth. I don't want to tell her because I'm
scared I would hurt her feelings. Every friend I know
says the same thing.

Needs Fresh Air

Dear N.F.A.,

You don't want to say, "Everyone talks about your elephant breath." But you could say, "As your close friend, I'm letting you know that I think you should brush your teeth in the morning." Too blunt? How about offering her a breath mint or peppermint? She turns you down? Look her in the eyes, and say with kindness, "I really think you should take one." You could also ask, "What's your favorite toothpaste?" or talk about some kid at camp who always had bad breath because she didn't brush her teeth.

Dear Carol,
My friend says my feet stink when I take off my shoes. I do worry that the smell drifts up.

Funk E. Feet

Dear Funk E. Feet,

Do you shower or bathe often, and do you wear clean socks? Your friend might just be giving you a hard time, so don't let her teasing undermine your self-confidence. On the other hand, don't rush to remove your shoes unless you're alone. Most adults would never dare.

Bathroom Talk

Dear Carol,
One of my friends always farts. She even does it on my pillow. She thinks it's funny. It's not. One of my

friends said that she farted sixteen times once at her house. I've tried implying that it's really gross, and I even gave her funny looks. Nothing works.

Smelled Out

Dear Smelled Out,
Yuck! Instead of giving her funny looks or implying that it's gross, say, "Go to the bathroom—don't fart on my pillow." When you think about it, you may be doing her a favor by letting her know that her loud lewdness is driving friends away. After all, what's funny to second-grade boys doesn't sell among older girls. Or older boys.

Dear Carol,
I am a heavyset girl with acne. I have only one friend and she's my cousin and my mom makes her be friends with me. Besides being not pretty and not popular, I have another big problem. I don't know how to say this, but I fart a lot. I can't help it. It just comes out at the worst moments like once in class when I dropped my pencil and bent over to pick it up. Everybody calls me the big fat fartmonster. I get sad a lot because boys think I'm gross. Please tell me what to do.

Miss Stinkypants

Dear Miss S.,
Things will get easier because as your classmates grow up, they will quit being deliberately cruel. As for flatulence, I do have some thoughts. Rich

and spicy foods are more likely to cause gas than lighter simpler fare. Try to eat slowly, and don't eat more than your body can comfortably digest. If you've noticed that cider or onions or beans get you in extra trouble, avoid them. Avoid soda or gum chewing if those add air to your system. Try taking Tums or a different antacid. And tune in to your body so you're not caught by surprise. When necessary, hold it in, and if it's too late . . . stay seated!

Dear Carol,
I'm in sixth grade and we have to go to the bathroom between classes because the teachers don't let you go during class even if you have to. Well, the girls' room is very crowded between classes and I just can't go when there are a lot of people around.
Prefers To Pee In Private

Dear Prefers,
I don't blame you, yet it's time to get used to sharing a bathroom. It's not good to hold it in forever, and every other kid in your class is in the same situation. Even presidents and princesses go to the bathroom, so try not to be mortified by what is normal and natural.

Dear Carol,
I feel weird asking this question, but when I use public bathrooms I pee really loudly. The splashing makes so much noise that it makes me embarrassed.

Especially at school, I hate using the girls' room when others are there. Trying to make myself pee slower doesn't work. What else can I do to keep quiet?

Too Loud

Dear Too Loud,
At home you can run the faucet to camouflage the sound. At school, when you gotta go, you gotta go. Please know that you are much more aware of this noise than anybody else. Instead of trying to pee more quietly, try to accept that you and your friends are mammals who drink and eat and pee and poop. I'm all for discretion about such matters, but since one often has to use the bathroom at school or in theaters or restaurants, I encourage you to forgive yourself for doing what everyone next to you is also doing.

Dear Carol,
My friend doesn't wash her hands after going to the bathroom. It's disgusting. Should I tell her? I don't want to embarrass her.

Clueless

Dear Clueless,
Many people don't wash their hands after using the bathroom. I'm glad you do! You can say something, though it might be awkward. Keep setting a good example and if you're ever about to bake together, speak up with a casual, "Let's wash our hands first."

Dear Carol,
I don't know what's wrong with me. Sometimes when I do a number two, I bleed. I don't have my period yet.

Worried

Dear Worried,
Ask your doctor, or better still, phone in your question instead of waiting and worrying until your next checkup. But let me ask you this: Are you getting enough fiber? If all you eat is pizza and rice and meat, it could be that you sometimes get constipated and that when you do finally, um, poop, it's a strain and that can cause a tiny tear. Eat Raisin Bran, veggies, and fruit, and drink lots of water (possibly even a half cup of coffee), and things may go more smoothly. By the way, your period has nothing to do with this.

Night Night

Dear Carol,
My problem is that I stay up way too late, usually until about 11 P.M. I get so tired that I fall asleep in the bathroom and at school and I am grouchy with my parents. Once I even fell asleep and drooled at school. Help!

Falling Asleep

Dear Falling Asleep,
Your body is desperate for more sleep. You may be a night owl, but since you have to fly around with the early birds at school, try to adjust your body clock. Get enough exercise in the afternoon so that you're physically tired, tackle homework early, and turn the TV and computer off by nine. Before bed, take a soothing bath, have a glass of milk or chamomile tea, and read, perhaps with relaxing music in the background. Avoid late-night cola, coffee, chocolate, spicy foods, arguments, or activity. Sleep is necessary, restorative, and pleasurable—so indulge. Instead of thinking, "I'm not tired yet," hop in bed and tell yourself, "I *am* tired and I'm glad I'm in bed." If you just can't tuck yourself into bed an hour earlier each night, go to bed extra early once or twice a week and try to sleep in on weekend mornings. Afternoon catnaps can make a difference, too—napping isn't just for little kids.

Dear Carol,
Do normal people touch their bodies before they go to sleep and is it all right to do that? My brother said it could kill me.

Wondering

Dear Wondering,
Your brother is mistaken. Some people touch

themselves and some don't and it is all right and perfectly normal either way.

Dear Carol,
I'm 12 years old and I'm ashamed to admit this, but I still wet my bed. My friends keep inviting me to slumber parties, and since I always say no, some of them think I'm stuck up. But I can't tell them the truth. I'd just die if anyone knew! How can I stop so I can go?
Bed Wetter

Dear Bed Wetter,
I've gotten lots of letters like yours. Bed-wetting actually runs in families. Many bed-wetters have a parent who was a bed-wetter. The condition even has a name, enuresis, and most pharmacies and grocery stores sell disposable absorbent underpants for just this reason. Talk to your mom about asking a doctor about treatment and medication. A doctor can prescribe a nasal spray that can help you get through a sleepover, slumber party, or even sleepaway camp. A doctor can also tell you about an alarm system with a beeper that can gently wake you up if you're about to have an accident. Meantime, don't drink much at night, pee right before you go to bed, and don't feel guilty—you will get through this.

Doctor, Doctor

Dear Carol,
Exactly what is a gynecologist? When do you go to one? I am too afraid to ask my mom.

Wants To Know

Dear Wants To Know,
A gynecologist is a doctor who specializes in the female body and knows about everything from menstruation to birth control to having babies. He or she has no male patients. Whereas pediatricians are experts on babies and kids, gynecologists know about women, young, old, and in between. You can start seeing a gynecologist now or during your teens, and especially if you have lots of questions about puberty or s-e-x. Then again, if you adore your pediatrician and he or she treats adolescents, there's no hurry to switch.

Dear Carol,
I'm feeling really uncomfortable about pelvic exams. I don't want to have one by a woman doctor but I don't want one by a man doctor either. Who would you prefer it by?

Confused

Dear Confused,
I have had good male and female gynecologists over the years. Ask an older friend for a recommendation. Remember that your doctor is doing

-103-

a job, not being a perv. When he or she is poking around to make sure you're healthy, you can be silently reciting the alphabet backward (ZYXWV . . .) or getting ready to ask all the saved-up questions you've been too embarrassed to ask your mom.

Dear Carol,
This kid in my class is going around telling everyone that I'm contagious. I have Lyme disease, but it's not contagious. I asked him to stop, but he won't.
                                                    Lyme Disease

Dear L.D.,
The boy will shut up and grow up and probably look back with chagrin at what an idiot he was. Meantime you'll get better in a hurry—I've been treated for Lyme disease, too. It is hard to deal with blabbermouths, but calmly say, "You get Lyme disease from ticks, not people, and it's not contagious any more than a mosquito bite or bee sting is contagious." (Though you may be tempted, try not to add, "DUH!!!")

Dear Carol,
I have been diagnosed with asthma. Most of my friends know and are really protective of me. I appreciate their concern, but I want everything to go back to normal.
                                                        Confused

Dear Confused,
Sometimes I wonder if there is such a thing as normal. If friends say, "Let's meet at your house because mine is full of cats, bunnies, and guinea pigs, and I know you're allergic," that would be thoughtful. But if friends try to hold you back from sports, that may be overprotective. Say, "Sports help me stay strong, and if I suddenly feel short of breath, I have medicine, so I just take a puff from my inhaler." Your friends are sure to have questions; answer them as clearly as you can. Let them know that you aren't sick, you just have asthma. If *you* have questions, call (800) 7-ASTHMA or visit the Asthma and Allergy Foundation of America online at www.aafa.org.

Dear Carol,
I have epilepsy and I take medications so I won't have any more seizures. I can handle it. But one of my closest friends always acts as if she worries I'm going to drop dead or something. She also worries she can catch it from me.

Sick Of It

Dear Sick Of It,
Reassure your friend that epilepsy is common but not contagious, and that thanks to the medication you take, your brain is unlikely to suddenly short-circuit meaning you're unlikely to

have a seizure. Tell her that when a person does have a seizure, she loses consciousness for moments or minutes—rarely forever! Find out more about your particular condition so you can let her know what to do if you did have a seizure. Say that if you ever swim together, a seizure could be very dangerous, but that ordinarily she need not worry. I'm glad you know how to take care of yourself, and I hope you can educate your friends (and teachers). To learn more or to find a pen pal with epilepsy, call the Epilepsy Foundation at (301) 459-3700 or check out www.efa.org.

Dear Carol,
I am going to have surgery and then I have to wear a back brace. I am afraid that all the girls at school are going to make fun of me because they already do.
Teased

Dear Teased,
I'm sorry you're going through this, though it will be well worth it in the big picture. As for the teasing, the best thing to do besides ignore the turkeys is to acknowledge them. When you get back to school, instead of looking downward and ashamed and priming yourself for victimhood, come up with a comment even before they do. Say, "Can you believe I have to wear this?" If a girl does tease you, say, "Yeah, this brace stinks."

Sometimes it disarms people if you fire the first shot yourself. Before you know it, the brace will come off, and you'll be and feel stronger. For now, the more comfortable you are with yourself, the more comfortable others will be with you. Look on-line for a chatroom where you can talk with kids having similar experiences.

Dear Carol,
My friends, my parents, and my doctor think I should get plastic surgery on my nose and ears, but I don't want to change myself for purely cosmetic reasons.
Big Nose

Dear B.N.,
What??! Unless I'm missing something, I'm with you. I admire your confidence and ability to stand up for yourself. There are many beautiful profiles and silhouettes, not just one! Would Barbra Streisand really have been better off with a dainty nose? Sometimes friends and even moms can be well-meaning but misguided, and while most doctors are trustworthy, some are motivated by money. Cosmetic surgery is an option that certainly makes sense in extreme cases or after terrible accidents. But if you like yourself as is, more power to you! Someday you may rethink all this, but there is no reason now to be rushed under the knife.

Dear Carol,
I want to get my tongue pierced or at least my nose.
My mom says some piercers don't know what they're
doing, and some people are allergic to metal jewelry.
What do you think?

To Pierce Or Not To Pierce

Dear T.P.O.N.T.P.,
I think your mom is right. But then, if my BFF
had a degree in pierceology and I was positive
that I had no metal allergies and she had sterile
equipment, I still would never let her put a hole
in my tongue. (How many holes does the female
body need?) Most girls can look great without
trying so hard, and less can be more when it
comes to beauty. If you're healthy and friendly,
you're probably looking good.

Pretty or Not, Here I Come!

Dear Carol,
I am blond with green eyes and I am slim. Friends and
strangers sometimes say that I could be a model.
Plainly put, I don't want it at all. I have literally gone
out of my way to look less modelish and beautiful. I
have gone without washing and brushing my hair, I
try to find plain and dull clothing, and I never wear
makeup. I don't want guys to notice me. I am in ninth
grade, so don't think the hormonal thing hasn't

kicked in yet. But is there any way I can let the world
know that this person is not available?

Help

Dear Help,
It's one thing to choose not to send out flirtatious signals. It's another to hide behind dirty hair and dull clothes. Why not enjoy the fact that you got lucky in the looks department? Why not figure out how to be attractive without making appearance your main playing card? Don't flaunt your beauty, but don't disown it either. Might there be other reasons why you run from attention? Think about it.

Dear Carol,
I am 13 and I think I am ugly. A lot of my friends say
I'm pretty, but I think they are just trying to be polite.
Do you have any advice?

Feeling Ugly

Dear Feeling,
Focus on your strong suits—what you like about yourself and what friends like about you. Instead of cursing yourself, work on improving your attitude and appearance. Talk to your mom (or grandmom?) about getting a haircut, sprucing up your wardrobe, or tackling acne or weight issues if necessary.

Dear Carol,
I have a best friend who's pretty but overweight. She thinks she's ugly and always tells me how pretty I am. I guess it's true, but I don't want her to feel bad when she's around me.

Feeling Bad

Dear Feeling Bad,
Do you feel bad when you're with a girl who is a better student or athlete than you? Do you feel bad when you're with a friend whose parents have a nicer car or fuller fridge? I hope not! We all got dealt different cards. If you're pretty, lucky you. Don't spend all your time in front of the mirror, but don't feel guilty about your looks either. Boost your friend's self-esteem by complimenting her on her strengths: "You are so funny!" "You are so amazing with animals." "You play the violin so well!" "You always know how to cheer me up." "You're a great friend." My hope is that since you are best friends, you can both figure out how to feel good—not bad—when you are together.

Friendship Frustrations

●●●●●

Carol and Judy and Jen. We met in sixth grade and we can still make each other laugh. We've gone to movies and parties and concerts. We've talked about everything, everything, everything. We've celebrated at each other's weddings and comforted each other in times of grief. Today we traded e-mails and it felt like we were back in school, passing notes. Girlfriends are for keeps. Which of your friends might be forever friends?

Popularity

Dear Carol,
It seems the only way to be popular is to be someone else, but when I try to be someone else, that

*someone is usually rejected, too. I just don't fit in
with others in the right way.*

Poppin' To Be Popular

Dear Poppin',
Instead of struggling to be popular, strive to have
one or two real friends. Which girls do you like
besides the most popular ones? Your next-door
neighbor? The girl behind you in English? The
new kid in school? Keep developing your strengths
(academic, athletic, and personal) and join an
after-school activity to meet new people. Then be
yourself—your most outgoing self. Say hi to lots of
kids. Ask questions like, "How was your weekend?"
and listen to the answer. If someone says, "My
weekend was fun—I went to my dad's," don't say,
"Mine was fun, too." Ask what her dad is like. Be
nice, not nosy. Instead of thinking about fitting in,
think about connecting to others. Friendship will
follow. Honest. And real friendship can last a lifetime whereas popularity can end at graduation.

Dear Carol,
*I am in the cool clique. It's more like a club. We have
two presidents (they are the coolest) and I am one of
them. Last week, a nerdy girl asked if she could be in
our clique. Two people said, "Give her a chance." Two
others said, "Are you kidding?" Now it's my decision. I
think we should give her a chance, but I'd rather eat
a tapeworm than lose my coolness!*

Coolest

Dear Coolest,
You want others to think highly of you. But you want to think well of yourself, too. And you want to be cool—not cold. How would you feel if you said no to that girl? How would she feel? Try not to be so exclusive. The coolest people are the warmest, most accepting, and most open to others. And the "nerdy" girl may turn out to be funny or thoughtful or smart once you get to know her. Besides, if you act exclusive and tides turn, people could start excluding you.

Dear Carol,
These girls in my school all live in big houses and wear new clothes. They are nice to me, but sometimes I think they are laughing at me behind my back.

Not As Fortunate

Dear N.A.F.,
No matter how much you have, someone out there always has more. Rather than dwell on what others have, look at what you have. Do you have a loving family? Close friends? Special talents? A great personality? You say you are not as fortunate, but money is not the only measurement. And girls with money aren't necessarily happier than girls without. I doubt these girls are laughing at you any more than you would laugh at a girl whose home is smaller than yours.

Dear Carol,
My friends are really great, and they all like me. My house is fun, and we have animals and a big barn. I always invite them over. But they never invite me to their houses.

Liked For Me?

Dear Liked,
You have great friends and a great house. What's the problem again? Oh yeah . . . Listen, if we were getting together, I'd rather hang out in your barn than my apartment. Sure you can tell your friends you'd like to go to their homes or meet somewhere. But since you described your friends as "great," try not to second-guess them or worry about being "used" or fall into the quicksand of insecurity. It may also be that your parents are more welcoming or easygoing than theirs. Believe me, if your friends didn't like you, they wouldn't be coming over at all.

Dear Carol,
I'm in eighth grade. Recently, I became friends with a popular girl and now she wants to set me up with her old boyfriend. I talked to him once, but didn't feel anything special. (I like another guy.) How can I tell her without ruining our friendship?

Friendship On The Line

Dear F.O.T.L.,
It would ruin your friendship if you said,

"Ewwww!" and trashed the guy. But if you say, "He's cute, but I didn't feel anything special with him," that should get you off the hook. Sometimes it's not what you say but how you say it.

Dear Carol,
I'm one of the most popular girls in my class and when my teacher says that we can have partners for something, a lot of people rush over to my desk to ask if I can be their partner. I always end up hurting someone's feelings.

Guilty

Dear Guilty,
Hitting the popularity jackpot does have its disadvantages—including disappointing potential partners, lunchmates, or partygivers. You can't be everywhere at once, but you can team up with a variety of people and you can say no nicely. If you say something like, "Sorry, I already have a partner—maybe next time?" no one has to feel hurt, and you don't have to feel guilty.

Dear Carol,
There is this group of popular girls. They are snotty and mean and they get the cutest guys. They love to exclude people and make fun of people. I'm getting so frustrated with them. I don't know. Maybe I just want to be popular and grow up faster.

Slow Grow

Dear Slow Grow,

If everyone stopped paying attention to the popular group, they wouldn't be popular, would they? Real friends are the ones who count because being able to discuss events and feelings with someone who listens is even better than just exchanging hallway hellos. It may seem pathetically slow, but you are growing up faster than you think.

Dear Carol,

In my seventh grade, there are three groups: Popular, Liked, and Geeks. I am liked so I am glad I am not a geek. But I want to be in the popular category.

Liked, Not Popular

Dear Liked, Not Popular,

I suppose if you look at it that way, I was in the Liked category too. Most students are! An advantage of not being Popular-with-a-capital-P is that you know your friends like you for you, not your status. However, if you long to climb the ladder, try studying (yes, studying) the popular kids. How do they act? Get beyond a one-word answer like "cool" or "stuck-up." What traits make popular kids appealing? Is it their self-confidence—and can you try to be like that but still be you? Is it their enthusiasm—and can you be more enthusiastic? Is it their way of looking right at the person they're talking to—and can you do that? By the way, some of the geeks you are ready to dismiss will blossom in ways that will leave some of the popular kids in the dust.

Dear Carol,
I'm not popular and I don't get it because I do what all the cool girls do, but I don't get anywhere. Some people say I'm a goody-goody. I have only a few people who are nice and are my friends.

Hopeless

Dear Hopeless,
If you have a few nice friends, you're not Hopeless—you're doing fine. Only a handful of kids are really popular, so don't consider yourself left out just because you're not in that one teeny-tiny group. Keep being yourself instead of just doing "what all the cool girls do." Join some activity (sports, service club, theater) to make more friends. And try not to listen to name callers. Anyone who still gets into name-calling doesn't exactly have her own act together, does she?

Dear Carol,
I'm in middle school, and a girl I've been friends with since kindergarten is in class with me. The problem is that I'm getting popular and she isn't and some of my new friends think she's a dork. I still like her, but she is getting on my nerves. I want to tell her that I don't want to be friends anymore but I don't want to hurt her feelings.

Ex-Friend

Dear Ex-Friend,

If you tell her that after over half a decade of friendship, you're ready to call it quits, trust me, you will hurt her feelings. Do you have to choose between an old friend and a popular friend? Aren't you allowed to have more than one friend and be friends with girls from outside one group? If not, who is not allowing this? (So what if your new friends don't like her— they don't have to.) There is no need to break up with a girl the way you might with a boy. But if you want to drift apart, consider calling less often, making fewer plans, and being less friend-ly rather than making a painful pronounce-ment. In other words, fade out of her life, don't stomp out.

Changing Friendships

Dear Carol,
I have this friend who acts like she knows everything in the world. She's usually nice, but she's so bossy sometimes. I don't know if I should like her or not, although I still do.

Hard Decisions

Dear Hard,

If you mostly like her, keep on liking her. It's eas-ier to have friends than enemies. If she's ever super bossy, say so. Stay open to other girls, too (sit with them at lunch, talk with them after school), and then pat yourself on the back for being tolerant—not a know-it-all.

Dear Carol,
How can I tell my friend that I don't want to be her friend anymore? Her parents are friends of my parents. When she phones, my mom says to talk to her, but I don't want to.

Needs Help

Dear Needs,
It's good to recognize which friendships make you feel good and which drag you down. But ask yourself why you are tired of her. Is this new dislike genuine or is it coming from other friends and not you? Can you ask your mom to plan adult get-togethers instead of making her friendship a family affair? My hope is that you and the girl can see each other less without your having to spell out the bad news.

Dear Carol,
I was best friends with this girl, but then she started thinking she was too cool for me. Now she ignores me. So I made new friends and started having fun with them. My mom just talked to my friend's mom and found out she wants to be my friend again. I don't know if I can trust her, and I can't leave my new friends. They are so good to me.

Now What?

Dear N.W.,
Just because a friend (new or old) enters your life doesn't mean someone else has to exit. If Miss Moody warms up to you again, fine. It's easier to be friendly than unfriendly. But don't leave new friends high and dry. You know how it hurts to be ditched, so why ditch girls who are good to you? Give the on-and-off girl a second chance if you want, but cautiously and without turning your life upside down. It's better to have more than one close friend anyway.

Dear Carol,
My very best friend just started going steady with an eighth-grader. We are in sixth grade. Suddenly she's really popular with other guys and snobby girls. I like the girls we used to hang out with but she's been giggling with other kids and acting as if I'm not even there. My mom says to forget her, she's an airhead, but how can I?

Frustrated

Dear Frustrated,
You can't. But you can say hi to, hang out with, phone, or e-mail other girls. You and your old friend may become close again. For now, however, focus on the people who are there for you. She may not be an airhead, but she is foolish and shortsighted to treat her best friend so shabbily.

Dear Carol,
Last year a girl and I were best friends. This year
we're in different classes, and she acts like she doesn't
know me. Today, in the hallway, I said, "Hi. I really like
your sweater," and she acted like she didn't hear me.
I didn't do anything to get her mad.

I'm Still Here

Dear I'm Still Here,
I'm sure you didn't, and that's why it can be so
puzzling and devastating when friendships
shift—which they often do in middle school.
Keep being mildly friendly, but if she stays high-
and-mighty, don't grovel. Get more involved with
the girls in your classroom, neighborhood, and
after-school activities. I hope your next best
friend has more depth and loyalty.

Dear Carol,
I'm in the sixth grade, and I still play with Barbies.
Recently my best friend told me she decided that
playing with dolls is "childish" and now she won't
stop bothering me about it.

Dollbaby

Dear Dollbaby,
Can you play with dolls when alone or baby-
sitting or with a younger cousin or neighbor?
With your friend, do other things: talk, walk,
take magazine quizzes, play board or computer

games. If she doesn't stop bothering you, say, "Give me a break. Friends don't have to like and dislike all the same things."

Dear Carol,
One of my best friends went to middle school and instantly started wearing makeup and acting like she's way too cool for the rest of us. It makes me ill. Should I say something?
Grossed Out

Dear Grossed Out,
I wouldn't. Everybody is changing at different speeds—physically and emotionally. Try not to dwell on her superficial changes, and hang out with others, too. She may come around.

Dear Carol,
I act silly with my friends, and they laugh, and we have fun. But now I want to take care of my looks more. I'm afraid that if I do, my friends might think that I'm acting like the popular kids we hate.
Silly

Dear Silly,
You can be silly and fun and also brush your hair and wear lip gloss. Your friends may be surprised if you alter your style, but so long as you don't become snobby, they shouldn't object. Friends don't mind if you grow up; they just don't want you to grow away.

Dear Carol,
My two best friends spent a lot of time together over the summer and now the three of us hang out, but they don't treat me the way they used to. I feel like an afterthought. They can't stand to be away from each other. They even have nicknames for each other.

Afterthought

Dear Afterthought,
You're not an afterthought. You're a close friend who used to be a best friend. Is there someone else who can become your best friend? Or can you be content to have several close friends? It doesn't sound as if the girls are trying to be mean, but it must be hard watching them be closer than ever. This whole picture could change if one of you suddenly moves or has a boyfriend or goes to a different school or even camp.

Dear Carol,
I have a good friend. But ever since another girl came to our school this year, it's been confusing. For example, at lunch my friend will be totally absorbed in the other girl's conversation. Then as soon as the girl gets up, my friend practically jumps around to me. As soon as the other girl gets back, I'm a nobody.

Nobody?

Dear Nobody?,
It sounds as if your good friend has two good friends. That does not have to be a problem. I

wouldn't call a showdown, but I would try to make friends with that other girl and with different girls. You can even tell your friend that you realize that you both are allowed to have other friends—but you sometimes feel jealous and don't like it when she acts like you aren't there.

Dear Carol,
I have this friend and I can never tell if she's mad at me or not but she gets upset if I ask her.

Never Knows

Dear Never Knows,
Stop asking, "Are you mad at me?" Just assume she's not and talk about things besides your relationship.

Dear Carol,
At my party, my so-called best friend wrote me a letter and it really hurt my feelings.

Hurt

Dear Hurt,
If you're still mad, call to clear the air and to find out which side of the door she is on. Start with "I" not "You." In other words, don't say, "You are such a jerk." Say, "I was hurt by your letter" and listen to her response.

Dear Carol,
My ex—best friend and I got in a fight, and she started

talking about my family in a way that ticked me off. I asked if she wanted to solve this after school. Later, outside the library, she said she was ready, but she brought a lot of friends. I said we should fight Monday and I'd have my people and she could have hers. The problem is that I don't want to fight—I'd rather talk it over. But I can't tell her that.

World War III

Dear World War III,
Why not? She probably doesn't want to get bruised and bloodied either. You aren't actors in an old Western; you're classmates. Of course talking it out between the two of you makes more sense than going to battle. Phone and say, "Let's call off the fight. This is stupid. I'm sorry we both got so mad. We used to be friends, and I don't want to be enemies." She probably feels the same way. If not, if she's intent on fighting, and you're genuinely and understandably worried, talk to your parents or a trusted teacher. (If you're ever feeling threatened or are scared that someone is downright dangerous, don't just lose sleep over it. Discreetly inform an adult who will take your concern seriously.)

Dear Carol,
This girl is having a huge holiday party and she invited everyone in the class except three people. I was one of them. She used to be my best friend.

Left Out

Dear L.O.,

Ouch! It stinks to feel excluded. You could write her a note that says something like, "If you wanted to hurt my feelings, you did, and if you want to change your mind, you can." Of course, it's posssssssible that your invitation got lost in the mail. If you decide to stay silent and accept that friendships can shift when you least expect it, then ask your mom to help plan something fun the evening of the party. A movie, play, or dinner with cousins? Who are your close friends now? Make future plans with them, too.

Dear Carol,

I've had this best friend since first grade. We used to run up to each other and tell each other stuff and start laughing. Now I'm lucky if she says hi in the hall. And she never says, "Call me," or anything like that. If I invite her over, she says, "Maybe, I don't know," then later says no and goes to someone else's house. At recess, we used to sit and watch the whole playground like we owned it. Now she and her other friend do that. I've tried telling her how I feel, and I even wrote her. It helps for a while, but nothing changes. Once I called her house and her sister said, "She's with——. They are best friends now." I hung up and sank to my knees and cried and cried. No one can ever take her place. She is my best friend always and forever. I won't hurt her like she hurt me. If she is not my best friend, there will be an empty place inside me that can never be filled by anyone else.

All Cried Out

Dear All Cried Out,

I'm sorry you're feeling so miserable. The bad news is that she has moved on. You've been friendly, you've invited her over, you've told her how you feel, and she's still not warming up. That stinks; that hurts; and sometimes that's life. Close friends don't always stay close friends. The good news is that there will *not* always be an empty place inside you. When you wrote, "She is my best friend always and forever," you were wrong. She was your best childhood friend. But you will have other middle-school friends and high-school friends and college friends and adult friends.

Instead of hovering around unwelcoming girls, hang out with people who make you feel good. Join an activity in school and find a summer job or program where you can meet new girls. Is there a counselor you can talk to about your hurt feelings and ways to make new friends?

Making Friends

Dear Carol,
I'm in seventh grade and I have a lot of friends in school but on weekends and vacations, no one wants

to be with me. I never get calls from anyone. I call my friends, but they are always busy. What am I doing wrong?

Lonely

Dear Lonely,
I doubt you're doing anything wrong. I believe in downtime, yet your friends may be genuinely busy with lessons, rehearsals, and sports, and you, too, may want to sign up for weekend soccer or summer camp. Try to figure out which of your friends you like most—and which like you most. With whom can you think aloud without worrying that she'll make fun of you? Who lives closest to you? Is there someone new in town or someone whose best friend moved or someone who just ended things with a friend or boyfriend? Invite that girl over. Instead of saying, "Are you free Saturday?" suggest something fun to do. Maybe your parent can help so you can say, "I'm having a party," or "We're going to a movie," or "Do you want to sleep over?" or "Do you want to go skating?" or "We have an extra ticket to —" Try not to make your loneliness obvious. I know that sounds hard and even unfair, but seeming sad scares friends off whereas seeming upbeat is more of a magnet.

Dear Carol,
I have no friends. I'd do anything for one good friend.

I don't want to sit alone at lunch. People say, "Just talk to someone," but it's not that easy.

Friendless

Dear F.,

It's not that easy, but it's not impossible either. Try these suggestions. #1. Notice if there is anyone new in school who may not have lots of friends yet and ask what she misses about her old school and likes about this one. #2. Say hi to at least four girls each day and try starting a conversation by saying "That test was hard, didn't you think?" or "Want a piece of gum?" or "Did you hear that . . . ?" #3. Join ballet, jazz ensemble, science club, yearbook, lacrosse, tap dancing, something! #4. Call someone at home and ask about homework. Talking on the phone can be easier than in person, and you can even scribble a few conversation topics down ahead of time—I'll never tell.

It takes courage, but if you are friendly (not clingy), and if you get to know people and let them get to know you, you will make friends. Keep noticing which girls seem happy to talk with you (versus the ones who act like they're doing you a favor) and which make you laugh (versus the ones who make you feel stupid). Then don't hang around the stuck-up crowd—even if they are considered popular.

Dear Carol,
I have about twenty or more online friends and I was
wondering if any of them are really who they say
they are. :) :(:*(:-) :-/ :-] :-[:-} :-o :>
;) :() :+0 :] :[:^) >:-) :x }:-$ [:-#
Fakers?

Dear Fakers?,
I like your faces, especially the last three—the
one whose lips are sealed, the one whose money
is where his mouth is, and the one with braces
who is wearing headphones. (I know my smi-
leys!) Do you ever exaggerate in the privacy and
anonymity of a chatroom? If asked your weight
and height and age and boyfriend status, do you
ever type with one hand while crossing your
fingers with the other? It's smart to assume that
some of your on-line friends are not as young,
old, experienced, innocent, rich, wild, or lucky
as they may say. On-line friendships can still
be fun, but *do* believe what you've heard about
never giving out your password, true address, or
phone number to a person who is, after all, a
stranger.

Dear Carol,
There are two girls who are really nasty to me. I want
to be their friend, but it is hard because of the way
they treat me.
Trying Hard

Dear Trying,
Maybe it's time to stop trying so hard with them and to spend your energy on other girls. Do you really want to be friends with girls who are nasty?

Dear Carol,
My family and I moved four months ago. We're about seven minutes away from our old house. Almost every night I cry myself to sleep. I miss the old neighborhood.

Homesick

Dear Homesick,
Wet pillows are the worst. Here's my advice: Phone the two or three friends you miss most and invite them over—to dinner or for a sleepover, individually if possible. They probably miss you, too. Make a habit of talking on the phone or on-line. But be friendly to new neighbors, too. You built good relationships in the past, and you can do it again.

Dear Carol,
What do you do if a friend you have been friends with for five years is moving? What can you do to keep it from hurting?

Sad

Dear Sad,
It will hurt, and you will miss each other. The hurt you're feeling shows what good friends you

were and are. You can also promise each other you'll keep in touch by phone, e-mail, snail mail, and/or visits.

Dear Carol,
My really good friend is moving. When she told me, I was sad, but I couldn't think of anything to say. I think I made her feel worse.

Left Behind

Dear Left Behind,
It's not too late to tell her that you feel sad and hope you'll always stay friends. She's probably sad *and* nervous, so keep her spirits up by telling her that she'll make lots of new friends because she's such a great person. Consider throwing her a going-away party or giving her a friendship ring or piece of jewelry. But hang out with others, too, because you don't want to feel left behind forever.

Dear Carol,
My best friend from school moved this summer. Every time I invite her over, she can't come. When I call, she talks about how much fun she had with her friends going to the movies and stuff. Every day I wonder does she have a new best friend?

Left Out

Dear Left Out,
Ouch. I'm afraid it does sound as if she has moved—and moved on. You two may become

friends again someday but right now, get closer
to girls who live closer.

Dear Carol,
*I want to make more friends but since I'm home-
schooled, I can't join any clubs. I might be able to join
swimming at the YMCA. But other than that, I can't
think of anything.*

More Friends

Dear M.F.,
Join swimming and see what else that Y has to
offer. Also look into a church choir. Or community service. Or local Girl Scout troop. Or yoga
class. Or group tennis lessons. Try to start a book
club at the library. Is there a bowling league or
Sunday pickup softball game near you? You may
have to make an extra effort, but you can find
friends.

Dear Carol,
*I am very popular with the boys but not with the
girls. I have friends. I just don't get along with girls.
Any advice?*

Boy-Friend

Dear B-F,
Some girls probably envy your ease with boys.
But don't lump all girls into one pile. Some girls
play ice hockey; some wear pearls; some do both.
Look for individual girls with whom you might

be compatible. Is there a girl on your team whom you can compliment on the field or sit with on the bus? Do you have a guy friend with a nice sister or girlfriend? Isn't there someone in class you can phone or e-mail? Since you can make male friends, you can make female friends.

Dear Carol,
I used to have a lot of girlfriends but then I became so jealous every time I saw them with someone else that I would get mad and try to break them up. After a while I lost my friends and things started to go downhill. Now I am good friends with this guy in school. There's one catch though. He's 29. Lately for some reason, he's been sort of ignoring me.
Missing A Friend

Dear Missing A Friend,
I assume the 29-year-old works at your school, and he may have realized (or been told!) that it is inappropriate for him to be your closest confidant. Sorry, but that is because too many young girls do get rushed and taken advantage of by older guys. I know you miss him, but try again to phone a former friend or plan something with someone new. You can give other girls and guys a chance—and you can remember to give them some breathing room, too.

My Friends Don't All Get Along

Dear Carol,
There are four girls in my school who are very rude.
When they have parties, they invite me but talk
about my friend behind her back. Should I tell her?

Confused

Dear Confused,
No, that would hurt. Next time others put her
down, consider defending her by saying, "I think
she's nice" or "You'd like her if you got to know
her." Believe it or not, they'll respect you if you
don't just sit there and let them rag on your
friend.

Dear Carol,
I have two friends who constantly fight. I'm right in
the middle. When one comes over, she draws mean
doodles about the other. They talk about each other
to me, too, then ask what the other said. Of course I
have to tell them. But I feel awful and guilty about it.
What should I do?

Guilty

Dear Guilty,
Get out of the middle. Tell each friend that you
like them both and you aren't going to be the
conveyer of mean messages anymore. You feel
guilty because you've allowed yourself to get

caught in the cross fire instead of calling a truce. "Of course" you have to tell a person she's been trashed? No, no, no. You never have to willfully hurt someone's feelings. Perhaps you enjoy knowing that these girls like you more than they like each other. OK. But instead of picking apart the absent girl's personality, just have fun with the one you're with. (Confession: Grown women sometimes gossip about mutual friends, too—but they know never to turn around and report it!)

Dear Carol,
I have three best friends. I'm closer to one than the others. Sometimes she and I talk about the other two. But I'm worried she and one of the others talk about me.

Upset

Dear Upset,
They probably do—and oh well, you can't have it both ways. While they may gossip, I doubt they're vicious. Besides, as Oscar Wilde put it, "There is only one thing worse than being talked about, and that is not being talked about."

Dear Carol,
My friends fight when I'm around. Now they are both asking me to be on their side. My mom says to stay out of it. Should I?

Stretched Like A Rubber Band

Dear S.L.A.R.B.,

Yes. If you choose, you may lose. Instead, tell your friends—separately or together—that you don't want to get sucked into this because you like them both. You can even add that you hope they'll make up. If you think one of your friends is wrong about something important, and you feel you should speak up, go ahead, then add, "But let's not fight anymore." You can also see them separately. It's good to have more than one friend, and twosomes often work better than threesomes.

Dear Carol,

My friends and I always get mad at one girl. She always calls me and asks me why we are mad at her and I don't know what to say because I'm only being mad because my friend is.

Staying With One Friend But Losing One

Dear Staying,

It's time to think for yourself instead of dumping on a girl without even knowing why. How would you feel if you were the odd one out?

Dear Carol,

Whenever my friend invites me to sleep over, she always invites another girl and we get into fights. My friend and I never fight when it's just us.

Sick Of It

Dear Sick Of It,
Can you invite your friend to sleep over at your home? Or suggest she invite you two on separate nights? Your friend probably wishes you could all get along, and if that happens, great. But if sharing her is too complicated and three is a crowd, stick to two at a time.

Dear Carol,
A girl in my class totally hates me for no reason whatsoever. There is no way to avoid her because she is a friend of my best friend. I don't want an archenemy so I don't know how to deal.

Mad

Dear Mad,
No reason whatsoever? She probably wishes your best friend were *her* best friend. You have two choices: Stop worrying about her or try to be civil. If you're friendly, she might stop thinking of you as a threat—and stop being in attack mode.

Dear Carol,
My friend likes a person I don't like, and I don't want to be that person's friend.

Mixed Up

Dear Mixed Up,
You don't have to. The point is not for everybody to like everybody. The point is for you to like a

few girls who like you back. Once everyone understands this, things get a lot simpler.

Dear Carol,
I've always had lots of friends from one group, but,
for instance, they like popular musicians and I like
Mozart, and they like soap operas and I like old
movies. Now I'm talking to girls in this other group.
They are more like me. Unfortunately, they are kind
of nerds. I still like them though. At lunch, I divide my
time in half. One day I sit with one group; one day,
the other. Well, both groups are getting fed up. I
would like them all to be friends but the first group
is afraid to be seen with the second group and I need
to pick.

Baffled

Dear Baffled,
The best thing about college and adulthood is
that you don't need to pick. You can have all sorts
of friends, and no one minds. While some so-
called nerds may not yet have the social skills of
their popular peers, they may have surprising
opinions and tastes and may prove to be loyal
longtime friends. I hope you can stand up to
everyone and hang out with whomever you want
whenever you want—even if your friends don't
all make friends with each other.

My Friends Can Be So Annoying

Dear Carol,
My best friend and I are very close, but this other girl is trying to butt in on us. She is trying to take away my best friend! What can I do?

Annoyed

Dear Annoyed,
You can act lukewarm, and she'll probably lose interest. But wait—is she really trying to steal your best friend or is she just being friendly? Your friendship isn't fragile, so there's nothing wrong with each of you hanging out with others.

Dear Carol,
I have a friend who is a "tag-along." Everywhere I go, there she is. At snack time, she is waiting at my desk. When I talk to someone else, she gets mad. She thinks she owns me. I've tried to tell her to stop bugging me, but I'm afraid I might hurt her feelings.

Too Close For Comfort

Dear Too Close,
It's nice to be in demand, but enough is enough. Even close friends need a little distance, and you are entitled to be with others. Next snack time, approach someone else's desk, or speak up. Instead of saying, "Stop shadowing me," say, "I like you, but I wish you wouldn't get mad when

I hang out with other people. I don't get mad when you hang out with other people."

Dear Carol,
When my friend calls, she always has another call. So she puts me on hold for five to eight minutes. When she gets back on the phone, she says she has to go because she wants to talk to the other person and she says she'll call me back, but she never does.

Bothered

Dear Bothered,
You don't need to be treated like yesterday's news. If she puts you on endless hold, don't put up with it. When she gets a call-waiting, say, "I'll let you go—I've got to go anyway." And stay on the lookout for girls who will value your time and affection.

Dear Carol,
My friend always calls me and goes on for hours about nothing. She never lets me say anything. How can I tell her she's wasting my time?

Bored To Tears

Dear Bored,
To end a phone call politely, you can say, "I have to go eat dinner now" or "My dad needs the phone." But since your friend hardly lets you get a word in, why not speak your mind rather than

go bonkers? Tell her conversations are supposed to be part talking, part listening, and she isn't letting you talk. If she can't or won't change and you choose to put up with her endless yak attacks, then listen on a cordless phone while straightening sweaters, sorting jewelry, filing your nails, or doing some other mindless task. She can't waste your time unless you let her.

Dear Carol,
Last night, my friend called me and asked if I liked this one girl. I told her what I thought of the girl, and it ended up that it was a three-way call. The other girl was on the phone and heard everything! What should I do?

Clueless

Dear Clueless,
Sometimes I'm so glad I'm a grown-up. Your so-called friend did you and the other girl wrong. You can apologize to the other girl or just hope that the conversation somehow evaporates. But as for your friend who placed the conference call, you can tell her that her high-tech move was a low-down trick. She is not trustworthy. Don't become her enemy, but don't rush to invite her over next time you're in the mood for company.

Dear Carol,
This girl in my class copies everything I do. I start wearing my hair in a bun; she wears hers in a bun. I

wear chokers; she wears chokers. I like a guy; she likes the same guy. She has been copying me for three weeks and nobody really likes her. I've asked her nicely to stop and she doesn't. It is driving me crazy! Nuts! Bananas! Up the wall! How can I tell her to get a life?

Copied

Dear Copied,
Imitation may be the highest form of flattery, but being copied gets old. She copies you because she looks up to you and is too insecure to figure out what to wear or whom to like on her own. To help her grow out of this, can you build her confidence? Compliment something she's wearing. Ask what guys she thinks are cute and if you agree, say so. (If you say, "Yuck!" she'll keep playing it safe by liking your choices.) Finally, think of it this way: Your problem is that she copies you. Hers is that she has few friends and little self-esteem. You have a better problem!

Dear Carol,
I just made a great new friend this year but she's always talking about her "best friend" and how she can't wait to see her. It makes me feel hurt.

Not The Best Friend

Dear Not The Best Friend,
She may not mean to hurt you. Roll with it, or go ahead, and say, "I know you have a best friend,

but it sort of hurts when you keep bringing her up."

Dear Carol,
This one girl keeps telling everyone we are best friends. She is my friend, but I don't want everyone to think we are best friends.

Annoyed

Dear Annoyed,
Say, "I feel awkward saying this, but I think of us as really close friends, not best friends." You can even add, "Labels like 'best friends' make me sort of uncomfortable." Better to speak up than simmer in silence.

Dear Carol,
I have a friend who always flirts. I am not jealous—just sick of it. She pays more attention to boys than girls. What's up with that? I'm not sure the boys even like her. Should I tell her or let her make a fool of herself? And how can I tell her that I am still on the face of this earth?

Totally Ignored

Dear T.I.,
Don't tell her that she's making a fool of herself (maybe she isn't, and besides, that would hurt). But do tell her that you wish she wouldn't act as if you're invisible whenever a boy walks by. If you want to talk one-on-one, her powers of

concentration may be best when you two are on the phone or on a walk or hanging out at one of your homes.

Dear Carol,

Among my friends, I'm the first to start everything: wear a bra, go boy-crazy, you name it. Whenever I talk about guys, my friends look at me funny and tell me I'm a freak. I'm not! Don't get me wrong. My friends are good friends. It's just . . . I don't know.

First Is Worst

Dear First,

It is difficult being the first or the last in the bunch. But be patient because friends can be out of sync, then catch up and appreciate each other again. If your old friends don't want to hear about boys, talk to them about other things and confide in your sister or cousin or a newer friend.

Dear Carol,

I have a friend who is not polite. She gets mad if I don't help her pick up around her house. What does she expect? I'm her guest!

Mad

Dear Mad,

Maybe her parents get mad when she has a friend over and the house is left in shambles. Why not be a polite guest? Offer to help clean up any mess you two make.

Dear Carol,
My friend brags so much that all my other friends hate her. She's a good friend otherwise, but I don't have the guts to tell her that I'm—
                                    Sick Of Her Stupid Lies

Dear Sick,
People who brag and lie are insecure. When you are happy, you have no need to brag. You could tell her that you like her best when she's being honest and not bragging. Or you could be less direct and say you like when people are sincere and that there was a girl at a party who was bragging and no one could stand it. (Maybe she'll get the hint?) Either way, consider complimenting your friend (yes!) so she can stop complimenting herself. Also, keep doing things that make you proud of yourself so you won't care when she acts proud of herself.

Dear Carol,
I have a friend who blabs every time I tell her a secret. Once I told her a secret about the parents of a different friend getting a divorce. She told everyone, and that other friend got mad at me.
                                    Big Mouth

Dear Big Mouth,
Can you blame her? Sounds like you're mad at your friend—and yourself. It's tempting to share

other people's gossip, but if you want people to tell you secrets, keep those secrets. No more blabbing to blabbers. If you are ever burning to let a secret out, consider writing it in a diary or a letter you never mail or talking with someone who lives far away. Meantime, if you can't keep a secret, expecting a friend to is a lot to ask.

Dear Carol,
My best friend came over last night. I said I'd be right back, I had to go to the bathroom. When I came back, I saw her reading my diary. I hid behind the door to see how much she would read, and she read the most embarrassing things. I said, "Hi!" so she would hear me. She put it away really fast so I wouldn't notice. The next day at school she started spreading my secrets.
Embarrassed

Dear Embarrassed,
Some best friend! Bad enough that she read your diary—downright cruel that she spread your secrets. If I were you, I would have popped out from behind the door then and there and said, "Excuse me, that's my diary!" It's still not too late for an apology. And it's never too late to make better friends. (P.S. Start hiding your diary behind your books or underneath your oldest art projects.)

Dear Carol,
My friend takes my money. She owes me $5 and now wants more. All the girls do this to me. They ask me for my money or my lunch. When I don't give them what they ask, they get mad.

Sick Of Being Nice

Dear Sick,
You can be nice without being the local bank, and you can be generous without feeling used. Say, "I'd lend you the money, but you already owe me $5." Or "I don't have any extra money right now." Or "I'm hungry—can't you get your own lunch?" Saying no to others can mean saying yes to yourself. You don't have to buy friendships, and if girls routinely take advantage of you, it's time to quit being the victim and start finding friends who treat you better.

Dear Carol,
My friend comes over and borrows stuff. My mom has lots of art supplies and this girl just takes without asking. She's costing us a fortune, but I don't know how to say no.

Really Annoyed

Dear Really Annoyed,
Learn. If you don't, you'll get taken advantage of at home, at school, by girls, by guys, and on the job. Next time she is over, tell her your mom has

forbidden you to use her supplies. Say it clearly—
without guilt or apology.

Dear Carol,
My friend is way into softball. I play, too. But softball
is the only thing she ever talks about. She always tells
me that her parents (the coaches) say she's the best
pitcher. She is well aware that I'm a pitcher, too—I'm
on her team! All my other friends are sick of her. She
brags and is too critical of how people play sports.
                                                    Frustrated

Dear Frustrated,
She may be good at sports, but she's not a good
sport. Since both her parents are coaches, she
may also think softball is the only game in
town—and the only way to win their praise. Deep
down, she probably feels hungry for recognition
and threatened by you. Even so, enough already!
Defend your other friends, whether they are
athletic or not, and tell the girl that you're glad
you have softball in common but you want to
talk about other stuff—movies, books, families,
school, whatever!

Dear Carol,
I'm in sixth grade. Last year I had a really good friend
who was in fourth grade. This year, she decided to skip
fifth grade and now all my friends and I don't like
her. She isn't as mature as we are, and she doesn't

like the things we do. All the teachers are easy on her.
And she thinks she's my best friend!

On My Nerves

Dear On My Nerves,
Students don't decide to skip a year or repeat a year. Teachers decide. I think she skipped because she is smart, and she was your friend because she is a decent person. She may not be as mature as you are, but is she so terrible? Imagine if you suddenly had to be an eighth-grader and your one eighth-grade friend turned her back on you. I realize you're in a tricky position. But so is she. And since you liked her once, I hope you can like her again—and at least introduce her to other sixth-graders so she can find new friends.

Dear Carol,
My friends and I are sick of this nosy girl. She always barges into other people's business and talks baby talk and is a shadow. Sometimes she even makes animal noises for heaven's sake. She is so annoying! Could she be considered a stalker?

Utterly Annoyed

Dear U.A.,
No. I assume she's unarmed and unhappy. It's hard to have to deal with such a person but even harder to be one.

Dear Carol,
Something bad happened to me a few years ago.
A few months ago, I found out that the same thing
happened to my best friend. The problem is that she
won't stop talking about it. I ask her to stop, but it's
like she doesn't know what that means.

Getting Reminded In A Bad Way

Dear G.R.I.A.B.W.,
Maybe your friend needs to talk about the incident in order to understand it, accept it, put it in perspective, and move on. Can you two talk together with a parent, teacher, or counselor who can help you see that the bad thing wasn't your fault? I know you want to just make the bad thing go away, but since you can't, I think confronting the past (rather than trying to suppress it) makes sense. But I agree, it would be nice if you and your friend could talk about other stuff, too.

Getting Teased

Dear Carol,
I'm fed up with my friend teasing me. I especially
hate it when she does it in front of her other friends
because they, of course, laugh. It makes me feel so
low! I can't do anything about it without hurting her
or making her angry. I'm a really nice person, and I
want to be nice to everyone.

Tired Of Her

Dear Tired Of Her,

You're worried about not hurting her or making her angry when she is hurting you and making you angry. On the phone, tell her you like her but don't like the teasing and you hope she'll stop. She won't? Ask yourself what's in this friendship for you. After all, there's nice and there's too nice, and I hate to see you being the chump. (P.S. While she doesn't sound like an ideal friend, she'd be even worse as an enemy, so tread carefully!)

Dear Carol,
My friend is always saying things that make me feel dumb, and sometimes she even hits me. She tells me I should hit her back or say something, but I don't want to.

Hurt

Dear Hurt,

Tell her you don't want to insult her or hit her back—you'd like her to stop insulting and hitting you. If she can't, find friendlier friends by getting involved in a whole new activity, whether it's chorus, track, karate, Students Against Drunk Driving, the literary magazine, or being part of a bake-sale fund-raiser or church car wash.

Dear Carol,
My ex—best friend has been calling me a wimp ever

since I went home early from her slumber party. I just
wanted to go home.

Not A Wimp

Dear Not A Wimp,
Lots of girls don't feel as comfortable at slumber parties as they let on. And it's low of her to call you names. If she's still calling you a wimp, say, "Give me a break," or go head-on with, "So I was a little wimpy. Get over it," or "OK, I'm not perfect—neither are you."

Dear Carol,
A girl at my country club is always making fun of me.
Our parents are friends, and some of the boys she
likes like me.

Teased

Dear Teased,
Whenever anyone makes fun of you, ask yourself why. This girl may be jealous because the boys she likes like you. Can you accept that and try not to let her jabs get to you? Focus on the girls and guys who like you.

Dear Carol,
My best friend calls me "Chunky." My mom doesn't
like it, but I really like this girl.

Puzzled

Dear Puzzled,

I'm with your mom. "Chunky" has an edge to it and whether you are or aren't overweight, there's no reason why your so-called best friend can't come up with a nicer nickname. Don't be shy about telling her so. After all, she wouldn't like it if you called her "Bean Pole" or "Jelly Belly."

Dear Carol,

I like a lot of sports (baseball, basketball, soccer), but girls at my school say I'm a tomboy. What do you think?

Tired Of Being Teased

Dear Tired,

I think you should enjoy as many sports as possible. Sports can help you be confident and healthy and part of a team. What's wrong with being a tomboy anyway? (I was.)

Dear Carol,

My mom buys me expensive clothes and I like them. Some of them are pink. When I wear them to school, the girls make fun of me. The thing that really bugs me is that they wear old hand-me-downs from brothers, sisters, and parents. Other people say I'm cute.

Fashion Conscious

Dear F.C.,

You don't like what everyone else is wearing and everyone else won't like what you're wearing. They shouldn't tease you, but nor should you feel that wearing something expensive is somehow superior to wearing something previously worn. My closet has expensive clothes and hand-me-downs, and I like both and feel good in both. It's possible that these girls are acting stuck-up because they think you're acting stuck-up. If you ever happen to be genuinely tempted to compliment one of them on her field goal or performance or campaign speech or handwriting, jump in, because a kind word may be the easiest way to dissolve hostility. Otherwise, try to not let them get you down and listen to your fans not your critics.

Dear Carol,
A few days ago, I was at my friend's house and we were playing and dancing weirdly. I started laughing so hard that I peed in my pants. I ran to the bathroom and when I came out, I told her what happened. When she was done laughing, she called a lot of people and told them.

Mrs. Pee Body

Dear Mrs. P.B.,
Some friend. I'm sure that in retrospect, you wish you had squelched the truth or stopped her in her tracks by saying, "Don't tell anyone. I'm embarrassed." At this point, the incident is probably ancient history, and speaking of, I'm sure plenty of Romans, Greeks, and Egyptians had accidents, too.

Dear Carol,
One time I was walking to my friend's house and as I stepped onto her porch, the door flew open and she came out crying with her mom behind her holding a leather belt. I ran home. The next day she made me promise not to tell a soul. I promised. But I told a friend and she told her friend and so on. Now my friend won't talk to me, and everybody teases her. What should I do?

Needs Major Help

Dear Needs Major Help,
You should apologize very sincerely to your friend in a note or in person. And you should get the other girls to quit teasing her by saying, "Look, it's bad enough that her parents are hard on her—let's not make things worse." You will all feel better if you start treating each other better. Next time you promise a friend you won't tell a soul, don't. (Telling an adult about abuse would not count as gossiping, but as trying to help. You may even want to encourage your friend to confide in a school counselor or call a hot line.)

Dear Carol,
My hair is very thick and curly. People call me "Fuzz Ball" or "Fuzz Head." Once some people put pieces of foam and paper in my hair, and since it's so thick and I couldn't feel it, I walked around for half an hour until they finally fell out.

Fuzzy Frankenstein

Dear F.F.,
Auugghh! What creeps! I'm sorry you have to go
to school with them. They will grow up. Still! Talk
to your mom or a hairstylist about the best look
for you, and tell your best friend to let you know
if anything like that ever happens again. Sometimes people don't realize that, though awkward,
it's a kindness to say, "Your button is unbuttoned,"
or "XYZ—Examine your zipper," or even "You have
something in your hair—let me get it out."

Dear Carol,
No one really likes this boy in school. People pick on
him, and I want to tell them to quit it, but I can't
because everyone will think I like him. I don't! But
just because he's geeky doesn't mean they have to
tease him, right?

Feels Sorry

Dear Feels Sorry,
Right. Kids can be cruel. But I get a surprising
number of letters like yours. Alone or with a
kind-hearted friend, tell the others you feel bad
for the boy. Say, "Give him a break. It's not like
he's geeky on purpose."

Dear Carol,
There is a rumor going around that this girl is gay.
She is my friend, but all my other friends don't like
her. Now there is a rumor going around that I am
gay. Even if she is gay, that won't stop me from being

her friend, and it shouldn't stop them either. One time, she and I and two other friends were hiding in a closet because my dad was chasing us and she was tickling everyone's legs and I didn't like it.

Confused

Dear Confused,
Some people are more touchy-feely than others and tickling girls' legs does not indicate that someone is or isn't gay. Lots of girls are affectionate together, but gay women are *sexually* attracted to other women. Even if your friend is gay, she may not truly know it yet. (Some gay women figure it out during their school years; others, not until later.) And you are right that she can be a good friend, gay or not. For now, rest assured that most rumors are short-lived and not taken very seriously.

I Don't Like What Friends Are Doing or Saying

Dear Carol,
I met this girl at my church. We decided to walk to a nearby mall. On the way, she stopped at people's doors and asked them to give money to some fund. If they did, she would pocket it. At stores she steals makeup and key chains. The other day she asked if I was mad at her. What should I do?

Law-Abiding Girl

Dear Law-Abiding Girl,
Keep your distance. If she asks what's up, say, "I don't like stealing." Who knows? She may have been stealing partly to impress you.

Dear Carol,
I just found out that a good friend of mine shoplifts. I was shocked when I saw her stuff a shirt we were gawking at into her purse. I don't think she knows I know. Should I turn her in?

Clueless

Dear Clueless,
Don't turn her in. And don't shop with her. But do talk to her. Shoplifting is illegal and in many stores, if she walks out with stolen goods, alarms will sound faster than she can say, "I didn't do it." Instead of bottling up your worries, express yourself—but to her, not the authorities. Don't write a note because someone could intercept it. Tell her, "I care about you and would hate to see you get into trouble." You may feel uncomfortable saying this, yet you already feel uncomfortable remaining silent. When friends shoplift or smoke or do drugs, your words may not turn them around—or they may make all the difference. Be a good friend and speak up. At least once.

Dear Carol,
One of my friends keeps telling me to try smoking.

It's a lot of pressure. Should I give in?

Nonsmoker

Dear Nonsmoker,
No! Most smokers start in their teens and later wish they could stop. Resisting pressure takes strength, and I'm glad you're not gung ho on taking up an unhealthy smelly addictive habit. The easiest way to say no is "Smoke gives me a headache," or "Smoking makes me cough," or "I don't like the smell." If you leave out the lecture (she's heard it), she won't resent you or stop being your friend. Maybe she'll even quit. There is such a thing as positive peer pressure.

Dear Carol,
My friend and this other girl were throwing spitballs on the ceiling of the bathroom. I know it's wrong. What should I do?

Needs Advice

Dear Needs Advice,
When you see someone doing something wrong, you don't have to do anything unless you think there is a danger. (In that case, get an adult!) But you could say, "You know, you're just making extra work for the janitor." Some girls get into trouble to impress their friends, so it's helpful if they realize that their friends are not impressed by, say, shoplifting, smoking, or spitballs.

Dear Carol,
I have this friend. Well, maybe she's not a friend. She always looks at my papers during tests and it is not fair.

Sick Of It

Dear Sick Of It,
If you don't want her to cheat off you, but don't want to report her, put your arms on your desk to block her view of your answers. You don't have to help cheaters—especially since so many are so good at helping themselves.

Dear Carol,
My friend is a plagiarist. She has copied a song, a book, and someone else's own story saying they're her own. Should I tell a teacher or her parents? I've already told my parents.

Confused

Dear Confused,
I wouldn't tell her parents. You might tell the teacher if you think he or she won't point the finger at you and won't immediately get your friend expelled. Your other alternatives are to keep quiet or, best yet, to talk to your friend directly. Let her know you've heard that song before and that you like her original work. She won't get away with plagiarism forever.

Dear Carol,
I got two of my friends in trouble because I told on
them for something they did that wasn't so friendly.
I don't think they deserved the punishments they got.
My teachers said I did the right thing, but I'm not
sure. I want them to know I'm sorry, but I don't know
what to say.

Tattletale

Dear Tattletale,
If you see someone carrying a gun or playing
with a knife or hurting a child or doing something dangerous, you would immediately tell an
adult. But when things aren't so clear-cut, consider the consequences first. Will the person you
tell on get kicked out of school? Will she turn
everyone against you? Has she been loyal to you
in the past? Sometimes keeping quiet is OK, and
talking to the friend directly rather than reporting
her may be even better. You didn't say what your
friends did, but if they already know you told on
them, maybe you can tell them you're sorry and
had no idea they would get in so much trouble. If
they don't know, I wouldn't race to confess now.

Dear Carol,
All my friends use dirty words and think it's cool
to call other people "retards." They also say "like"
every other word.

Stuck With Dumbmouths

Dear Stuck,

I'm glad you know words have meanings and that you aren't lazy with language. As for your friends, some people (including peers, interviewers, potential dates, and bosses) will be turned off by their speech, so I hope they try to clean up their act. While some friends can offer each other pointers and it's no big deal, for others, even well-intentioned suggestions can hurt without leading to change. How would your friends react to constructive criticism?

Dear Carol,
The boys in my class are racist. What they say is extremely rude. When I ask them why they make fun of people of different races, they say, "Why do you care?" I can't stand it anymore.

Confused

Dear Confused,

It is hard to stand insensitive ignorant people who make racist comments. It is also hard to change people. I commend you for trying to help others take off their blinders and see that there are good and bad people of all colors and backgrounds. Maybe it will make an impression on your small-minded classmates to see that slurs can lose them the respect of someone like you. If someone ever e-mails you a racist joke, reply with "That's not funny; it's racist," or "That's not my idea of humor," or simply one word such as "Lame" or "Sophomoric."

Dear Carol,
Two of my mom's friends recently died of AIDS. I loved them. My friends at school constantly say things that aren't nice about people who are gay. I know they are wrong, but I don't know what to say. Please don't tell me my friends are not good friends, because I switched schools and need all the friends I can get. I just wish people wouldn't make fun of people simply because they have different ways of living their lives.

Can't Get Over Them

Dear Can't Get Over Them,
It's hard to get over the death of someone you love. You lost two close friends, and your grief is a tribute to how much you cared about them. I won't say your classmates aren't good friends. But if they make ignorant and mean-spirited remarks, they do need to learn more about tolerance. Maybe you can help. Tell them they are too smart to be prejudiced. And tell them about your two friends who died. Although you can no longer talk to them, you can still talk about them.

Trying to Help Friends

Dear Carol,
This guy was my best friend and then he moved. He wrote me a letter telling me he's on drugs and in a gang!

Drug-Free

Dear Drug-Free,
Write and tell him you hope he's taking care of himself because you liked him just the way he was—off drugs. Writing him will help you feel better and may help him, too. Tell him it's a lot easier to get in a gang than out, easier to start a bad habit than end one. Be supportive, not a nag. Drugs can not only mess up his body, but they're illegal. You might suggest that he make an anonymous confidential phone call to get advice, information, and help. He can try (800) COCAINE (they'll answer any drug questions) or (800) 999-9999 (they offer support in any crisis) or (800) NCA-CALL (which is the National Council on Alcoholism and Drug Dependence, and is also reachable at www.ncadd.org).

Dear Carol,
I'm 15. I don't take any drugs, but I'm worried about my friend. He told me he used to smoke pot but has quit. I shouldn't worry anymore, right? Wrong. I do worry and here's why: He told me he quit after talking

to *his* mom because *his* smoking upset her—not because he realized that smoking was bad for him and he had the desire to quit. When he first told me about his former addiction, I freaked out. I even cried. I should probably just mind my own business, but I'm afraid he might start doing pot again. My parents had hard times when they were teens due to drugs, and I just don't want my friend to suffer addictions like they did.

How Can I Help?

Dear How Can I Help?,
Keep being honest with him and your good attitude may rub off. But give him the benefit of the doubt. There is a difference between having smoked pot and being addicted. Though I see your point, whether he swore off pot because of his mom or you, the key thing is that he quit.

Dear Carol,
My best friend and I are very close but she has such low self-esteem. She's always saying things like, "I'm dumb" or "I'm so ugly." Then she says that I'm "pretty" or "smart" or "lucky." It annoys me because she's a great person! I think she insults herself just so I'll give her a compliment. How can I help her?

Worried

Dear Worried,
Your company and compliments, respect and affection are helping. But you're right—it's a

shame she spends so much energy putting herself down. You might mention that the only thing you don't like about her is that she's constantly dissing herself. In fact, why not make her compliment herself and say, "I'm a good friend/singer/writer/artist . . ." right in front of you? You could also suggest she join an after-school activity or talk to a school counselor.

Dear Carol,
I have a friend who I think is depressed. She's always negative and talks about killing herself. She takes it out on other people and that makes it hard to be around her, so not too many people get to know her. The few of us who do regret it. I've found myself slipping into depression. I want out of this friendship but I'm concerned about how it would affect her so I've stuck around.

Worried Friend

Dear Worried Friend,
A tough one. First of all, it's important that you take care of yourself—that you eat well, get enough sleep, see peppier friends, stay involved with others, etc. But since you're already in the thick of things with this girl, keep taking her seriously. Tell her that she doesn't want to end her life, she wants to change her life, and she can do that. Encourage her to see a therapist and to sign up for extracurricular activities (maybe ones you're not in). And tell a trusted adult or

counselor or teacher about your concern for your friend and the bind you feel you're in.

Dear Carol,
My older sister and I are very close, and I am very good friends with her best friend. My sister's friend is very self-destructive. She cuts herself with sharp objects, has had problems with anorexia, and smokes—and she's only 14! My sister is afraid she's going to kill herself. We're trying to help but her suicidal attitude is scaring us and we can't tell either of our parents because then they wouldn't let us even look at our friend and she needs us right now.
Saving A Friend

Dear S.A.F.,
She's lucky you and your sister care. Tell her, "Promise me you won't hurt yourself," and make her promise to call you if she gets desperate. If you can't talk to your parents, can you talk to hers? Or another adult? This is too much for you and your sister to handle, and your friend needs therapy. If your school has a counselor you like, tip her off discreetly. And tell the friend to get some help or to at least call the Covenant House nine-line at (800) 999-9999 next time she's tempted to hurt herself. Sometimes at 14, it's hard to believe that life is long and that happier times are ahead.

Dear Carol,
I have a friend who is totally obsessed with poking herself in the finger and watching herself bleed. I really think I should tell her mother, but I promised I wouldn't tell anyone. I am afraid that if I tell, it will ruin our friendship. I am also afraid that if I don't tell, she will become more harmful to herself.

To Tell Or Not To Tell

Dear To Tell Or Not To Tell,
Tell. Staying quiet is hard for you and isn't helping her. Consider calling the mom during school hours and asking her to please not tell that you phoned. Then voice your concerns and suggest that the mom could just happen to notice her daughter's finger and could talk to her about the cuts.

Dear Carol,
I have a friend who just found out that her mom's an alcoholic. She has been for the past seven years, and her family is getting help for her. My friend doesn't seem to care, but I can tell she's hurting inside. I try to comfort her, but I can't.

Cluelessly Comforting

Dear C.C.,
You could ask your friend how she's feeling. But don't press, and don't gossip about her family to mutual buddies. Just continue being the

thoughtful nonjudgmental friend that you are. Whether she opens up or not, I bet she appreciates knowing you're there.

Dear Carol,
A friend's parents are getting a divorce. Should I tell her I know how she feels?

Broken Home Kid

Dear B.H.K.,
I wouldn't say, "I know how you feel," because how can any of us really know how someone else feels? But in a private moment, you can say, "I'm sorry about your parents. It must be hard for you." You might add something like, "When my parents split up, it was awful at first, but then . . ." and share any advice about how you got through it. Just listening to your friend and letting her talk will help her.

Dear Carol,
I have a friend and last week I was at her house and her mom slapped her in the face. Should I tell someone?

Concerned

Dear Concerned,
I don't think you should dial 911, although you may want to talk it over with your own parents. I'm opposed to slapping (and spanking), but that's how some parents discipline their kids,

and slapping (and spanking) are not illegal or life-threatening. If you knew a friend was being hit (as in roughed up or bloodied) or sexually abused, it would be important to report this to an adult.

Dear Carol,
One of my best friends was shot and killed in an acci-dent. He was in eighth grade. He and two of his friends were at his house and they found his older brother's gun in a shoe box. His friend was holding the gun in the air. The gun went off, and my friend was killed instantly. Please tell me what I can do.

Scared

Dear Scared,
What a sad letter. And what a tragedy—for the boy's brother and parents, and for all his friends, including the one who picked up the gun. I'm not surprised you feel scared and I can't believe how casual people are with guns! What was a loaded gun doing in that boy's home? In a shoe box, no less? Do you have other friends who have guns lying around? Many parents buy guns for hunting animals or hurting robbers, but since accidents happen and people get angry or reck-less, statistically, unarmed families are safer than armed ones.

It's very hard to lose a friend, even harder when the friend dies from carelessness. What has your school done to remember him? Set up a scholarship in his name? Dedicated the yearbook to him? Started a gun-control or safety-awareness seminar? If your school hasn't done anything—or enough—talk to the principal with suggestions.

You can also write your friend's parents. It doesn't have to be a fabulous letter. Just a note describing how he was such a friend to you. You'll feel good about sending it, and they'll appreciate receiving it. I hope this accident also helps you and others be aware of what a blessing life is.

Dear Carol,
Two days ago, a girl in my seventh-grade class died in a car accident. Everybody is a wreck. I wasn't very close to her, so it didn't hit me so hard that I cried all day, but I did cry. I'd like advice on how to help other people recover.
Sad Helper

Dear Sad Helper,
I'm so sorry for the girl's family and for your whole community. Her death will leave a permanent mark on her closest friends. It may make some think about (and value) their own lives more and it may leave some feeling heavy-hearted for a long time. Everyone grieves in different ways. Your classmates who feel terrible are allowed to feel terrible, while the kids who knew her less well need not feel guilty about smiling

and flirting and joking in the hallways. Don't avoid the saddest kids. Include them in on regular conversations, and if you ever feel like it, in a quiet moment, say, "You must really miss ——." Perhaps your school can honor her memory in a formal way or establish a scholarship in her name. Perhaps teachers can have a service, plant a tree, or ask everyone to write or draw something for a book in the library. Mourning takes time. This girl will never be forgotten, but someday even her friends will be able to think about her with affection and not just wrenching pain.

Dear Carol,
I have a friend whose dad has cancer. She always has breakdowns in school, and I do not know what to do about it. She will not tell me what's wrong. She says "Nothing," or "Family problems." All I want to know is how to find out what's wrong.

Helpless

Dear Helpless,
What's wrong is that her dad is sick and she is sad and scared. Instead of asking, "What's wrong?" say "This must be so hard for you," or "I wish I could help," or "You must be so upset," or "Let's take a walk," or just talk to her about homework or music. Put yourself in her shoes instead of taking her silence personally. Even if she doesn't feel like talking, she'll know she can turn to you if and when she does want to open up.

Dear Carol,
My friend's mom just died a few months ago. When-
ever she comes over, we like to gossip. Somehow the
conversation always leads to my mom, and my friend
gets a sad look in her eyes. I can tell she misses her
mom and I want to comfort her but I don't know
what to say.

Needs Advice

Dear Needs Advice,
Your friend will always miss her mom. You're not
reminding her of her loss—she's thinking about it
all the time right now. Since you are her friend,
say what's on your mind. Say, "I know you miss
your mom and I wish I could comfort you but I
don't know how." Give her a hug if she cries. Tell
her she can talk with you or cry with you whenever she needs to. And give yourself a gold star for
not avoiding your friend during this terrible time.

Dear Carol,
I have lots of friends. My best friend's father just died
and so now my other friends are saying I'm hanging
around her too much. No matter how much I pay
attention to them, they say I'm ignoring them. I think
they should cut her some sympathy!

In The Middle (As Usual)

Dear I.T.M. (A.U.),
I'm with you! The poor girl is hurting, and your
support is probably a lifesaver. I'm surprised

your other friends don't get it. If they usually need more than they give back, ask yourself if they're asking too much. And continue to be there as much as possible for the girl who lost her dad. In the big picture, friendships get reshuffled often, but a father dies only once, so I'm glad you recognize that your best friend needs you right now. My dad died many years ago. He was a wonderful man and he was my biggest fan and I still think of him every day— and I'm still grateful to the friends who were there for me during those long months when I almost forgot how to smile.

The Whole Boyfriend Thing

• • • • •

Have you started noticing guys? Or started noticing that other girls have started noticing them? Now is when boys—those creatures who until recently were either invisible, dorky, gross, or just ordinary folk—suddenly begin to look, well, better.

I remember my intense crushes on David, Billy, Jimmy, Norm . . . and that was before I even met Bob, my first real boyfriend.

Buckle up—these are bumpy years!

Oh Boy!

Dear Carol,
I have a MAJOR problem. Lately I've been getting a

crush on every male Homo sapien who is anywhere
near my age and anywhere near cute. What's wrong
with me?

Boy Insane

Dear Boy Insane,
Nothing's wrong with having lots of crushes so
long as you are still getting homework done and
keeping up with friends and family responsibili-
ties. Many girls feel hungry for romance, and
your honesty is refreshing. But try to be selec-
tive—not just desperate.

Dear Carol,
I'm 12 and everyone in school is talking about going
with boys. I like them and I would want to go with
them but I don't see what you do in a relationship at
this age.

Confused

Dear Confused,
It's true that many couples who are "going out"
aren't actually going anywhere. They're too
young to drive or meet at a restaurant. So they
talk, hang out, watch videos, do homework, trade
e-mails, and just get to know each other better.
Many couples don't even go that far. Others hold
hands, hug, and kiss. Please know that most 12-
year-olds have not paired off and you're not the
only one feeling confused.

Dear Carol,
My friend asked if I'd go out with him. I said yes. When I got home, I told my mom, and she started saying, "Go where? How will you get there? I don't want you dropped off by yourself!" She gave me a lecture on how she didn't start dating until she was twenty, so I told him no, and now no other boys will ask me out.

Dateless

Dear Dateless,
It's not too late to tell your mom that "going out" mostly means going public with the fact that you and a boy like each other. If you still care about the boy you turned down, explain the mix-up. If you want to see each other outside school, ask your mom if he can come to your home. Even if she says no, you'll still be dating before twenty.

Dear Carol,
My friends are interested in boys. I'm not really into them. When I'm around boys, I feel like I can't act silly or goofy. Should I pretend to like boys?

No Clue

Dear No Clue,
Nope. There may come a time when you feel more comfortable around all guys or certain guys. But since girlfriends often last longer than boyfriends, it's perfectly fine to be hanging with the girls.

Dear Carol,
Whenever I'm around boys, I become really shy or I
say stupid things.

Could This Be Like?

Dear Could This Be Like?,
You and almost every girl in your grade! Guess
what? Boys get nervous and tongue-tied, too.
With time, it will be easier to relax around boys
in general—though you may continue to feel
weak-kneed in front of a crush. For now, I doubt
that whatever you say seems stupid to anyone
else, so don't be hard on yourself. If you anticipate feeling shy in the lunchroom or at a party,
think ahead about topics of conversation or questions to ask. Notice what you talk about with
friends (teachers, pets, homework, television,
music, sports, books, camps, vacations, weekends, boys, and clothes) and discuss the same
stuff with the opposite sex (maybe leaving out
boys and clothes). You can also compliment a
guy on his shirt or ask how he got that little
scar.

Dear Carol,
I recently went to a mixer and I danced with one
cute guy all night. But I ran out of conversation ideas
so half of our night was totally silent as we danced.
What are guys interested in?

Silent And Scared

Dear Silent And Scared,
Guys and girls are often interested in the same things, from computer games to Olympic games. The most natural conversations sometimes come from discussing the here and now. Say, "This mixer is more fun than I thought it would be." Or that you like the music/deejay/punch/decorations. Or that you like the way he dances or that it's weird to see the gym all decked out. Or that you remember the first time you heard this song because . . . Guys need to work through their shyness, too, so don't feel that silences are all bad or all your fault.

Dear Carol,
I'm 13 going on 14. I'm not very interested in boys and I never will be. The reason why is—I don't really want to write this but—I think they are perverts. You should see my class. The boys say the sickest things about the girls.

Eighth-Grader

Dear Eighth-Grader,
I'm sorry you know so many rude and crude boys. When girls and boys get nervous, some act shy—and others act out. Many of these obnoxious types will eventually figure out how to talk about girls more respectfully. Meantime, never say never. A few guys will mature sooner than you think and others probably already disapprove of the loudmouths in your grade.

Dear Carol,
I like three boys and don't know which to pick. Once
I decide on one, the other two pop into my mind and
then I have to start all over again.

Love Stuck

Dear Stuck,
Who said you're allowed only one crush? Legally, you can have only one husband at a time. But crushes? The sky's the limit. Get to know all three (without flirting too much!) and don't pressure yourself into deciding. Think too about how each feels about you. The choice may soon become clear.

Dear Carol,
I once cried in front of a boy I liked. He hasn't said
anything to anyone, but I still feel really bad about it.
How can I live this down?

I Cried

Dear I Cried,
You've already lived it down. Give yourself a break. Boys get upset, too, and you're allowed to have emotions. Who knows? He may have been charmed that you felt safe enough to show your feelings.

Dear Carol,
I've been friends with this boy ever since we could
crawl. But this new girl moved here and now he talks

to HER all the time. I see them everywhere together and it's like he ignores me. I'm super-duper-mondo-jealous and I'm crying right now even as I write. I think I like him as a friend, but why am I jealous? Do I like him for more than a friend?

Is This Love?

Dear Is This Love?,
It can hurt to see someone you care about care about someone else, and while you may not love him, it sounds like you wouldn't have minded going out with him. Middle-school relationships are often short-lived, so you two may still have a chance at romance. For now, forgive yourself for feeling jealous and distract yourself by making plans with girlfriends and your family.

Dear Carol,
I've been lying to my best friend. I told her that I have a totally cute boyfriend. I even lie to myself because I can't stand the thought of not having a boyfriend. I also think my friend won't like me if I don't lie, but in my heart I know she'll still like me. Help!

Upside-Down Life

Dear Upside-Down Life,
If you are honest, she'll probably like you even more. And if you want to quit lying, you can. The truth is easier to tell and remember, and girls and guys will trust and confide in you more if you don't lie. (You don't seek out people who lie

and brag, right?) As for lying to yourself, please realize that most girls don't have boyfriends. Can you appreciate what you do have? Try.

Dear Carol,
My friend is pretty, sophisticated, and a big flirt. Whenever we're around boys, I feel invisible. I join in and joke but the boys' attentions are always on her. When she's not around, boys are nice to me.
Dull and Boring 13-year-old

Dear 13,
Some people shine in class, some shine in sports, some shine at parties, and a few people shine everywhere. Having a friend whom boys notice doesn't make you dull or boring. Think about where you shine. And think about this: many boys would prefer a genuine girlfriend than a first-class flirt. Having a popular friend has disadvantages—it's hard not to feel pangs of jealousy, and advantages—it's easy to meet the boys and girls she attracts.

I Wish I Had a Boyfriend

Dear Carol,
What's wrong with me? I don't have a boyfriend! I am almost a full-blown teen but nothing's happened. Most of the girls in my grade have boyfriends. I'm pretty and I don't understand. It seems everywhere

I turn, I see people hugging, holding hands, even kissing.

Lovely But Lonely

Dear Lovely But Lonely,
First of all, though couples do stand out, I can almost guarantee that most girls in your grade do not have boyfriends. If you made a list of girls and next to each wrote the name of her boyfriend (official boyfriend, not big-time heartthrob), you'd see that all your classmates haven't found soul mates.

Second, being pretty helps get you noticed, but only if you are visible. Invisible girls flock together, sit quietly, never talk to boys, and wonder why boys don't talk to them. Visible girls are friendly, approachable, and willing to say hi or initiate conversation. So while guys notice looks (just as girls do), they are drawn to girls who smile and sparkle and take an interest in them. Be likable and friendly and patient, and before you know it, someone you care about will care about you.

Dear Carol,
What do I have to do to get a boyfriend around here? Every time I like a boy, he never likes me back. I have never had a true boyfriend before, but I want one really bad. I feel like I'll never have a boyfriend.

Boyfriendless

Dear Boyfriendless,

I remember feeling that way, and I assure you that you will have a boyfriend, then another, then another. I hope you'll eventually find a person wonderful and caring enough to share your whole life with. For now, ask yourself why your relationships have been one-sided. Are the boys you like the same boys everybody else likes? (Yes? That makes it harder for them to single you out.) Do you talk with them, joke with them, get to know them? (No? Then how are they supposed to fall for you?) Another way to have more success on the romantic front is to take down your WANTED: BOYFRIEND sign and zero in on one or two available guys who enjoy your company. You're looking for a person, not a status symbol.

Dear Carol,
There is this girl in my school who is pretty and popular and all the guys drool over her. I wish they would get over Miss Perfect and notice me.
Still Single

Dear Still Single,

Some of them eventually will. Meantime a lot of guys probably wish the girls would quit drooling over the soccer star or the new hottie in class. There will always be eye-catchers who get more than their fair share of attention. But if you pay attention to boys who aren't used to celebrity treatment, you won't be overlooked for long.

Dear Carol,
*Every single boy I ever go out with I dump or stop
liking after about three days. Sometimes I even cry
over crushes and when I finally get the chance to
go out with them, I dump them immediately! Do
you have any advice on how to choose the right
crush?*

I Like Him . . . I Like Him Not

Dear I Like Him . . . I Like Him Not,
Having a crush can be easier and more exciting
than having a boyfriend. It sounds like you're
not quite ready for a true relationship—and
that's fine. But slow down before you pick up
then drop another guy because you don't want to
hurt their feelings or get yourself a bad reputation. Get to know your crushes instead of putting
them way high up on a pedestal from which they
can't help but fall. Someone who cares about you
and shares your interests is better boyfriend
material than someone who is simply cool, cute,
or popular.

Dear Carol,
Do guys like girls with braces? Please answer.

Left In The Dust, But Not For Long?

Dear Dusty,
Yes. Guys like girls with braces. Guys like girls
who like themselves and like them.

Dear Carol,
I've asked out every boy in my school, even younger kids. Everyone says no. What's wrong with me?

Needs A Life

Dear Needs A Life,
So get a life—not a boyfriend. Boys (like girls) want to feel special, not like #27 on someone's list of prospects. Instead of asking anybody else out, get to know the guys and girls in your school. And get to know yourself. What are you good at? What do you enjoy doing? What activity can you join? Grow as an individual before striving to be half of a couple. Can you talk to a teacher, counselor, or relative about how to make your life fuller?

There's This Guy I Like

Dear Carol,
I am really crushing on this guy who is so cute. I want to tell him I like him, but I don't want to make a fool of myself!

Boy Nuts

Dear Boy Nuts,
Don't tell him—show him. Instead of putting him on the spot and trying to get him to go public with his feelings, get gutsy and just say hi and

smile. Compliment him. Sit by him. Touch his arm ever so lightly. Look into his eyes. Use his name. Ask if he did the book report or saw what happened in homeroom. Notice if he's smiling back and holding up his end of the conversation. If he is, keep up your interest. If his mind is elsewhere, accept this and cut your losses. (Who needs an inattentive unenthusiastic boyfriend anyway?) Don't be in a hurry to spell out your feelings because it forces the guy to state out loud whether he likes you back (this can embarrass him) or doesn't like you back (this can embarrass you). He may also need time to figure out his feelings. Sending and reading subtle signals makes more sense than cross-examining your crush, and also gives him a chance to think about you.

Dear Carol,
I have this deep crush on a cool kid at school. He's popular, nice, and funny, but I can't find the right time to tell him. He knows I like him, but he makes fun of me, and the whole school knows.

Boy Crazy

Dear Boy Crazy,
You can't find the time to tell him what? That he's acting mean? He may be cool, but not to you. Why join his fan club? Since he knows you like him, stating it more obviously will not help—and might make it easier for him to keep making fun of you.

Dear Carol,
I really like this boy at school. Before he knew I liked him, he was really nice to me. Now he just ignores me. He's very cute, and he used to be funny, nice, and charming. It's been over four months. He hasn't told me why he doesn't like me yet.

Boy Problems

Dear B.P.,
And he probably never will. I'm sure he doesn't dislike you. He may just feel uncomfortable with you now that he knows you like him. Maybe he's not ready to have a romance in front of the whole school. Maybe the chemistry isn't there (meaning he likes you but doesn't *like*-like you) and he doesn't want to lead you on. Maybe his feelings have changed. Maybe they'll change again. Maybe he has a girlfriend elsewhere. For now, try to set yourself free to notice other guys.

Dear Carol,
Whenever I see this guy, I get this tingly feeling in my stomach, and I can feel my face get red. I want to ask him to go with me. But what if he says no? How can I get the strength to ask him? Also, should I be myself?

Love Everlasting

Dear L.E.,
Always be yourself—your best self. But before asking him out, get to know him better—and let him get to know you. If you rush to ask him out,

you run the risk of his turning you down. If you pretend you're someone you're not, you run the risk of his being disappointed when he finds out that you're not as into show tunes or car engines or horse races as you led him to believe. I know you're eager to make your move, but relationships that start slowly sometimes last longer. Find the courage to look him in the eyes, compliment his sweater or pet or goal, laugh at his jokes (unless they're lame), ask about vacations or homework or activities, and show that you bask in his attention.

Dear Carol,
I met this guy in orchestra and we always slap high fives and say "Hey" in the hall. I like him and I think he likes me. We'd be perfect together, but I'm afraid that if I ask him out he might say no and then our friendship would be demolished. I'd rather have him as a friend than nothing at all. What should I do?
Unsure Of Love

Dear Unsure Of Love,
Proceed with caution. It sounds as if things are all systems go, but there's still no need to lay your cards on the table. Keep deepening the friendship and consider flirting—without going overboard. Give him a chance to feel his feelings before pressuring him to voice them aloud. Say, "You sounded better than ever today," and smile right at him. Sit next to him and have your knee

gently brush his. He's keeping his knee next to yours? You may have sparked a romance. He's pulling away? At least you haven't put your friendship in jeopardy.

Dear Carol,
I really like this boy. I think he is poetic. Everyone else thinks he's a dork. I think he likes me, too, but he acts like he's afraid to say anything. We're good friends and I want to say something but every time I'm about to, I get pains and cramps in my stomach. I'm having all these weird dreams that he's in. Is there something going on with my hormones and how can I tell him how I feel without barfing?

Nice And Queasy

Dear Nice And Queasy,
Puberty isn't just about body changes; it's also about realizing that boys can give you butterflies—not just cooties! But don't rush to tell the poet how you feel. Enjoy your relationship as it evolves. As for disapproving friends, who would be going out with him—you or your friends? They may soon see what you've seen in him all along.

Dear Carol,
This really cute guy said he would go out with me if I looked like this other girl. I feel hurt, but I like him. He's sort of a player.

Sunken Heart

Dear S. H.,
He may be cute but he's also rude. No wonder you feel hurt! Why should you look like someone else? Question: Is he worthy of your admiration? Sometimes Cupid is stupid.

Dear Carol,
I love, I mean, love this boy, but how can I tell if he likes me? Sometimes he talks to me for no reason at all.
Helplessly In Love

Dear Helplessly In Love,
Does he look you in the eyes when he talks? Does he get flustered around you? Does he smile and laugh and ask questions and pay compliments? These are good signs! Some guys are charming to lots of girls, which is one reason why there's no foolproof way to read a guy. Keep getting to know each other.

Dear Carol,
I REALLY like this boy at school. Two years ago, I sent him three Secret Admirer letters. Then I sent him a fourth and told him that I was his Admirer. I know he remembers them by the way he acts when I pass him in the halls. Is there any other way to show him I like him? My friend says I should give him the "sad puppy face" and pay less attention to him so he gets "a taste of his own medicine."
Lovesick And Devoted

Dear Lovesick And Devoted,
Of course he remembers the letters just as you would if you had received three out-of-season valentines. You've made your feelings LOUD AND CLEAR. Now it's his move. How does he act in the halls? Happy to see you? Or annoyed and embarrassed? He knows it would be safe to tell you he likes you, yet he hasn't. This means he's not ready or willing to be your boyfriend—at least not now. The good news: He's not the only boy in town. Should you pay less attention to him? Yes, but not just with the hope of reeling him in. As for giving him a "sad puppy face," who'd want to go out with a sad puppy?

Dear Carol,
I have a humongous crush on this boy. I'm short and skinny and have damaged hair. I don't think he likes me. I've asked him and asked him and still he gives me the same answer. This is probably a stupid question but here goes: Should I ask him again?
Skinny, Short, And Have Damaged Hair

Dear Skinny, Short, And Have Damaged Hair,
You could be shapely, tall, and have lustrous hair and I'd still say: Nope. Hang on to your pride and move on. Just because girls can speak up in ways they couldn't decades ago doesn't mean persistence always pays off. This boy isn't drawn to you. A different boy might welcome your atten-

tion. (P.S. Since your hair bothers you, use conditioning shampoo or have a stylist cut it.)

Dear Carol,
I did something really stupid. I sent my crush a blatant love note with my initials on it, and I'm the only one in school with those initials. He stopped talking to me. To make matters worse, at a school fundraiser, we were playing Truth or Dare, and someone dared me to go onstage and say, "I love———!" and I did. Everyone heard me and now he stays away from me completely.

Boyfriend Tiger

Dear Tiger,
You embarrassed him by coming on too strong. It's not the end of the world, but it may be the end of your chances with him, at least for now. Next time don't go public with what should be private. Boys aren't toys—they're real live people with feelings. If someone who was not your boyfriend announced his ardor over the loudspeaker, you, too, might be mortified. Fortunately, the whole episode is probably water under the bridge.

Dear Carol,
I have a crush on my friend! He lives across the street.

Love Struck

Dear L.S.,
Uh-oh. Instead of feeling happy and relaxed, you feel excited and self-conscious? Instead of talking about anything at all, you find yourself jittery and empty-brained or blathering about nothing? You're not the first girl to fall for a friend—or the boy next door—but it can be awkward. Since friendship often outlasts romance, don't rush your crush or declare love. Do phone him and be slightly more flirtatious and complimentary than usual. If things work out, great! If not, your crush may fade, and you can still be friends, maybe even forever.

Dear Carol,
I want to go out with this guy but he calls me a dog and says things like, "It was a full moon last night, why weren't you out howling and going woof woof?" I try to keep my cool, but it's getting to me.
Wistful Thinking

Dear Wistful Thinking,
Why do you want to go out with him? He sounds more rude than romantic. Granted, maybe he's a funny friend who likes you but is too immature to express this more tenderly. But while waiting for him to grow up, can you get more involved with friends who don't degrade you?

Dear Carol,
There's this guy I like at school. He's popular and he

laughs a lot. But I really like my cousin, too. You can talk to him about personal stuff and he is so easy to talk to, it's like he's a girl! He also gives advice without making fun of me. I think he cares about me as a cousin and as . . . well, you know. When I see the boy in school, my heart starts pounding. When I see my cousin, I feel that I'm flying. What should I do?

Queen Of Hearts

Dear Queen Of Hearts,
It's wonderful that you and your cousin get along so well, and he'll be in your life forever, at holidays, weddings, and reunions. But when cousins kiss (or break up), Thanksgiving gets awkward. Cousin marriage is also taboo—and often illegal. Be friends and confidants, not sweethearts. Your bond with your cousin will always be safe, and if you feel a little jealous of each other's future dates, that's natural. As for the classmate who sets your heart to pounding, good luck!

Dear Carol,
I'm in love with this really radical guy. He has a great personality except he steals and smokes. I am not like that. We flirt a lot. What should I do if he asks me out?

Bad Boy Lover

Dear B.B.L.,
If you were comfortable about all this, you wouldn't have written me. "Bad boy" types can

seem exciting, and some girls think vice is nice, but smoking is bad for your body and stealing is against the law. It may be easier to put on the brakes now than later.

Dear Carol,
I'm 15 and I need your advice. My parents are racist and my boyfriend is black. My parents do not approve!

Color Blind

Dear Color Blind,
You don't need your parents' approval, but it does make things easier. Usually when parents don't like a girl's boyfriend, I ask the girl to think about why. Does he smoke, drink, do drugs, act rude, skip school, phone too late? Can she see their point? And what does she like so much about him? In your case, if your parents are prejudiced, they are not judging your boyfriend but have prejudged him—and found him wanting. Is that fair? Absolutely not. I'm glad you judge people by who they are and not how they look. But let me warn you, it's not easy to change parents. So you have three options. You can break up (especially if things begin to fizzle anyway); you can arrange for everyone to meet and get to know each other (harmony not guaranteed); or you can underplay your romance so you don't further upset your parents (remind them that you're going out, not getting married). If things

stay serious, keep asking yourselves the hard questions. Marriages between people of different races, religions, and backgrounds are increasingly common. But breakups and divorce are common, too, and keeping a relationship going is hard even in the most idyllic circumstances and even when all parents approve.

Dear Carol,
I like this guy who is 22. I am 13. Am I stupid for liking someone so much older? My parents don't like me calling him. Who's right?

Crazy Crush

Dear C.C.,
You're not stupid for liking him, but I'm with your parents. At your age, even a few years age difference is too much. You're a girl; he's an adult. You might want to think about kissing—going to "first base." He might want to go all the way—with or without regard to protecting you from pregnancy or sexually transmitted diseases, let alone emotional turmoil and hurt. Maybe he is flattering and harmless. But what if he's not? Do not meet him alone. Your parents are not being overprotective. They are looking out for you. (Picture the reverse situation. When you're a woman of 22, can you imagine hanging out a lot with a boy of 13? Why or why not?)

Dear Carol,
I have a total crush on my neighbor's little brother.
He's eight and I am 14. I haven't told her yet. Should I?
                                                    Brotherly Love

Dear Brotherly Love,
When you're 14, one year in either direction is
no biggie. But six years? That's a huge age gap.
Do you really have a crush on him or do you
think he's adorable? Do you want to hold hands
with him or baby-sit him? I wouldn't tell your
neighbor lest she embarrass you by telling classmates. If you think your feelings toward this boy
really are romantic, talk with an adult you trust
(perhaps a therapist or guidance counselor)
about fears you may have about growing up.

Dear Carol,
This may sound dumb but I have a huge crush on my
English teacher. He has an amazing smile. I feel like I
am not normal. I bet other girls don't dream about
their teachers.

                                                    School Daze

Dear School Daze,
I bet they do. I did, and I've received many letters
like yours. It's normal and natural to have a soft
spot for a teacher (he's a smart grown-up who
likes and respects you), and it's fine if those feelings provide a reason to look forward to school

each day. But keep your crush in check, because if a teacher (or adult coach) ever actually kisses a student, it's trouble for everybody. Why? Because you are underage and relationships aren't considered consensual when one person is in the power position. Keep enjoying those smiles, but protect yourself from growing up too fast and protect him from getting fired. In other words, don't schedule too many one-on-one tutorials!

There's This Guy Who Likes Me

Dear Carol,
People in my school told me that a boy likes me. At first, I didn't think it was true. But he has been sitting near me and smiling and stuff. It's kind of nice being able to say that a boy likes me, but I don't know if I am ready to have a boyfriend. I don't even know if I like him.

Boy Trouble

Dear B.T.,
Just because a boy likes you doesn't mean you have to like him back. Take your time figuring out your feelings. Do you feel all warm inside when he smiles at you? Do you look forward to seeing him? Do you think about him when you're apart? Or is there a part of you that dreads seeing him and wishes he were paying less attention to you? There is no rush to like him or any boy.

Dear Carol,
I have a huge crush on this one guy. I think he might like me, too. At a school dance, he danced the slow dance with me and his hands started out resting on my waist but by the end his hands were overlapping and he was holding me a lot tighter. I don't know how to tell him that I like him. Once he asked if I liked him and I turned beet red, and said, "No, just as a friend." Should I tell him?

Confused

Dear Confused,
He may be confused, too. Your lips said one thing—your face said another. Since your answer may have discouraged him, and you didn't mean what you said, you might want to try to show him that you care about him. And though I don't usually advise stating feelings early on, you may want to say, "I like you," or "I like being with you." You could also enlist a friend to talk to him for you, but such strategies often backfire. Or just wait for the next dance and hold him tight!

Dear Carol,
One day in science, I felt something pulling my hair. I turned around and the boy who sits behind me was rolling it up on his pen. In music he sometimes plays the recorder right in my ear. He is annoying, but he is also really cute. Does this mean he likes me or just wants to be funny?

Annoyed With Love

Dear A.W.L.,
What do you want it to mean? If you like him, smile and beam. If not, tell him to cut it out! Figure out whether you want to flash him a green light, yellow light, or red light.

Dear Carol,
There are two cute boys at camp. One sits near me sometimes, and I think he likes me. The other one, when I stare at him, says, "What are you looking at?" I think he likes another girl. Which one should I like?

Love Bird

Dear Love Bird,
You like two guys. One is nice back and one isn't. If you want a two-way relationship that makes you feel good, pick the guy you like who likes you. Why choose a guy who isn't choosing you? What kind of a boyfriend would he make?

Dear Carol,
There is this guy who rides the school bus with me. He's made it clear that he likes me. I don't know if I like him. Last year he hurt two of my best friends emotionally. Plus, he's not that smart and he has stayed back four times. I normally get A's and B's. He also picks on my little brother.

Confused About Feelings

Dear Confused,
What's confusing? You haven't said he's funny, thoughtful, handsome. You've said that he has hurt your friends, failed school, and been mean to your brother. It's one thing to repeat a grade, another to stay back four times. And it's one thing for *you* to pick on your brother, another for him to do so. Don't talk yourself into liking a guy who doesn't seem all that likable.

Dear Carol,
There's this boy who has liked me since first grade. He keeps asking me out. I have to make up excuses every time he asks me. I'm running out of them. What should I do to get him out of my face without hurting his feelings?

Excuse Maker

Dear Excuse Maker,
Since he has been unable to read the writing on the wall, you may have to spell things out for him. Next time instead of saying it's your grandmother's birthday (again!), tell him you are sorry but you aren't interested in going out with him and would rather just be friends. Gentle honesty is not rude—and can be kinder than leading him on.

Dear Carol,
This boy asked me out. Since I didn't like him, I said

NO! Then these seventh-graders told me to go out with him. I still said NO! I don't feel bad for him even though he ran off crying. Did I do the right thing saying no twice to his face?

Wonderer

Dear Wonderer,
It's always OK to say no. But be kind. "Thanks, but I don't really want to go out," may hurt, but not as much as "Are you kidding?," "As if!," "In your dreams!," "Yeah, right," or "No way, José!"

Dear Carol,
There's a boy in my class who keeps e-mailing me. He asked if I liked him. I said as a friend. He sent me another one and asked why I didn't like him. I told him I would rather not say. He keeps sending me more and more mail. I don't know how to tell him without hurting his feelings.

Hopeless

Dear Hopeless,
Since you've tried to let him down easy, your best bet may be to e-mail him again, and say, "Stop writing me so much. You're a good guy but I don't have special feelings for you. Sorry." You could even add, "I'm not going to open up anything else you send." Will you bruise his ego? Possibly. But bruises don't last forever.

Dear Carol,
I am really nice to everyone at school. Since I am
always smiling, I attract really weird guys. I have been
asked out three times this month. How do I stop
attracting these weirdos without being mean?
                                    Geek Main Attraction

Dear Geek Main Attraction,
Geeks often have excellent taste and some grow
up to be surprisingly cool. Don't stop being nice.
But do make sure you aren't giving off the wrong
messages. For instance, complimenting a guy's
jacket while maintaining several seconds of eye
contact might give the guy the idea that you like
him, not just his jacket. There's a wide arc
between nice and mean, and you're learning
how to be cordial without coming on strong at
the same time as the boys are learning to decode
female behavior. Things will soon be easier for
everybody. Until then, you can't always make a
guy stop liking you any more than you can make
a guy start liking you.

Dear Carol,
My best friend is a boy, and I found out he likes me a
little. I just like him as a friend. Now I don't know how
to act around him.
                                    Just Want To Be Friends

Dear Just Want To Be Friends,
If possible, try to act the way you always have. If

necessary, say, "I like you tons—but as a friend." And if you must, spend more time with other girls and guys. My hope is that his feelings will cool down (unless yours warm up), and you'll be able to keep enjoying your friendship.

Dear Carol,
I like this one boy and he likes me so we are basically ready to go out. But a lot of other girls like him, too, and they might hate me for it. Should I go out with the boy but risk my popularity?
                                    Needs Boyfriend Help

Dear N.B.H.,
You can have a boyfriend and keep your friends. You just have to be sensitive about it. Don't act stuck-up or talk nonstop about him or dump your friends in order to spend all your time with him. Do keep up your hobbies, interests, grades. Girls may envy you but they won't hate you.

In Love or Obsessed?

Dear Carol,
I met a boy last summer and I can't get him off my mind. I think I love him. My mind says like, but my heart says love.
                                    Like Or Love

Dear Like Or Love,
Love means different things to different people. I
think love is a heavy-duty time-tested two-way
street. Seems to me you're attracted to him and
like him a lot. Have you seen him since summer?
Do you dare send a postcard or e-mail? Are any
of your friends his friends, too?

Dear Carol,
I met this boy at camp. After camp ended, I realized
how much I really like him. I will probably never see
him again because he lives far away. He was perfect:
cute, athletic, smart, and kind. I feel like I'm obsessed
with him. I don't have his address, but I do have four
photos.
                                            Out Of Luck

Dear Out Of Luck,
You're right: Unless you're headed back to camp,
you probably won't see him again. So why spend
more time pining over him than you did talking to him? Try to put an end to your one-way
yearning. If you must, write his name down on
a piece of paper and dwell on him for a full and
lovely minute (or several), but then that's it—
make yourself think about other people and
things. I suppose you could drop him a note
care of the camp. But let's be realistic: This boy
was your first big crush—not your last. Get busy
with your here and now (school, friends, family,
activities) and check out the guys who live near-

by. Some of them are cute, athletic, smart, and kind, too. But no one is perfect—and neither was the camper.

Dear Carol,
I've had a crush on a boy for seven years. When we were in first grade, we were kind of boyfriend and girlfriend. We were in the same class for three years but then we were separated. Now, in eighth grade, we don't even talk or wave or anything. It's as if he doesn't even remember me. I can't stop thinking about him. I think about him every second of every minute, every minute of every hour, every hour of every day. I would talk to him, but I'm too chicken. Please don't tell me I'll get over it. I've been hearing that for years.

Completely Crushed

Dear Completely Crushed,
First grade was a long time ago. I won't say you'll "get over it" any more than a smoker would suddenly get over cigarettes. You need to make an effort to yank out Cupid's arrow or at least to talk to the boy so he's a person instead of a fantasy, and so you know where you stand. Don't be chicken. Say hi, smile, ask, "How are things going?" He'll either be nice and your daydreams will have some substance, or he'll be cold and you'll have a reason to chase thoughts of him away. Force yourself to focus on others, too—

female and male. Baby-sitting or doing a sport or practicing an instrument or joining the debate team or volunteering somewhere would be a better use of your time than thinking about a guy who may not be thinking about you. Once you get this boy behind you, you'll have room for real back-and-forth relationships that involve caring and conversation. Sighing over him has become a habit. If it's fun, fine. If drooling is a drag, next time he wanders into your mind, say, "You! Out of there!"

Dear Carol,
I have a huge obsession that's taking over my life. I'm in love with a famous actor. I have four huge posters of him, two thick books on him, and a million framed pictures of him. His face is all over my room. I think about him constantly. When I'm at school, I get all dreamy and stare into space. I write about him in my diary, pray for him in my heart, and frankly, live for him. I know millions of girls have crushes on him, but his soul is nestled so deeply in my heart that no ladder could be long enough to let him climb out. I don't want to let him go. I have dreams about him every night, and, when I wake up, I stare at his posters for twenty minutes. I cry for hours at a time because I know I'll never meet him. If he were close to death, I would give my life for him. I love him SO SO SO SO SO much. I write stories and poetry about him in my journal. But he'll never meet me. He'll never meet me. When all the

girls are crazy for another guy, I'll still love him with all my heart. My love for him is as boundless as the sea, my passion as deep as the North Atlantic. My heart is a rose pierced by his thorn of charm, sweetness, and amazing talent. He is the most perfect being in all creation. Oh by the inconstant moon, I swear! I love him so dearly, it hurts. Carol, what am I to do? It breaks my heart that our relationship shall never blossom. And I shall never again be happy knowing that I'll never meet my one and only love.

Aching Breaking Heart

Dear A.B.H.,
I hear you. I get it. The guy's in your heart and on your walls. But just as girls who have had royal crushes on royal princes have gone on to hook up with mere mortals, you, too, will survive and be happy again.

If you are enjoying all this mooning and swooning, fine. But can you rein it in a bit? Remind yourself that you'd be nuts to give your life for his and that you have no idea if he's really sweet—though I'm sure he's not perfect. Is this longing worth hours of tears? You're a romantic and my hunch is that you're in love with love as much as you are in love with this particular actor. Perhaps someday you'll be a romance novelist. For now, though, try to keep your feet on the ground.

Should Friends Get Involved in Each Other's Love Lives?

Dear Carol,

I have a friend who likes this boy and he likes her, too. The thing is, they are both a little shy around each other so I have to do all the talking for both of them. I end up feeling like a messenger. How can I get them to talk to each other so I don't have to do it for them?

Messenger

Dear Messenger,
If you don't enjoy being the go-between, bow out. Say, "Sorry, tell her/him yourself. I don't want to be the messenger anymore."

Dear Carol,

I have liked this boy for the longest time. He finally agreed to go out with me. But two days later my good friend told me that he only said yes to get me off his back. Should I be upset, forgiving, what?

Heartbroken

Dear Heartbroken,
Feelings don't play by the rules. The question isn't: How should you feel? It's: How *do* you feel? Upset, forgiving, what? Also, what he tells you counts more than what he tells her or what she says he told her.

Dear Carol,
My friend can snag anyone her heart desires. She goes out with different guys at once and sometimes it is my guy friends she does this to. Should I tell them?

Upset

Dear Upset,
Not if you want to stay her friend. It's not ideal to be the bearer of bad news. In fact, in the olden days, kings sometimes killed messengers.

Dear Carol,
My friends have big breasts and it's OK being like that, I guess, but now my best friend has a boyfriend. And I am worried that her boyfriend is just interested in her breasts and not her. How can I tell her this without hurting her?

Worried For Friend

Dear Worried,
I wouldn't step into another person's romance unless you know something dangerous is going on. In this case, you don't know what he's thinking. He may appreciate her curves, yes, but he may also like her spirit and smile just as she may like his looks and personality. If your friend seeks your opinion or may be in danger, speak up. Otherwise, mum's the word.

Dear Carol,
I have a friend that got asked out by a boy I know.
But they never went out. Now this boy hates her guts.
And he wants me to tell her because I'm her best
friend. But if I tell her, I'm afraid she will feel really
bad because she really likes him. What should I do?
                                                    Frustrated

Dear Frustrated,
Tell him, "I'm not going to tell her that." By the
way, *hate* is a strong word, so I hope the two of
them can continue revising their relationship.

Dear Carol,
I have this friend who is totally antiboy. I once slow
danced with a boy and she flipped out. She started giv-
ing me a hard time, saying stuff like "I can't believe you
did that!" Why does dancing have to be such a crime?
                                                    Confused

Dear Confused,
Dancing is not a crime. I don't know if your
friend is afraid of growing up or afraid you'll
grow up and leave her behind. You are entitled to
dance with whomever you want.

Dear Carol,
I met a boy in chorus last year. Whenever I go to
a football game, I see him there. My friends run up
and tell him I adore him. He sometimes gives me a

strange look or just smiles. How do I get my friends to stop embarrassing me and not hurt their feelings? How do I get my crush to notice me more?

Fed Up With Friends

Dear Fed Up With Friends,
For better or worse, your friends have already done a bang-up job of getting your crush to notice you. If you want to call them off, now's the time. Say, "Please don't run up to him anymore. It's enough and it's embarrassing. You'd feel the same way if I told your crushes how much you adore them."

Dear Carol,
I had a friend ask a boy to go out with me. His eyes sparkled, but he said no.

Crushed To Pieces

Dear Crushed To Pieces,
He may come around, especially if given a chance to get to know you (not your friend). He may already like you but not want to tell her. Enough of the he-said-she-said. Start talking to him, not about him. But if his eyes don't keep sparkling, don't crowd him with affection.

Dear Carol,
I told a guy in my class that I liked his friend. He screamed it across the cafeteria, and a lot of kids heard. I want to teach him a lesson. What should I do?

Embarrassed

Dear Embarrassed,
Usually the best thing to do after being humiliated is . . . nothing. Silence and discretion will make this situation smaller instead of bigger.

Dear Carol,
I have a problem . . . well, duh! I'm going into sixth grade and on the last day of fifth, I told EVERYONE that I liked this one guy. (Even him!) But over the summer, my feelings changed. When school starts, I know everyone is going to tease me or ask if I still like him.
Made A Huge Mistake

Dear M.A.H.M.,
You had a crush, not a contract. You told him you liked him, not that you would marry him. You are allowed to change your mind. The whole thing may be forgotten, but if someone asks, just say, "My feelings have changed" not "I can't believe I ever liked such a dork!"

Dear Carol,
I think I'm falling for my best friend's brother. My friend and I have been friends for more than three years and I have never had this problem. I can't talk to him the way I used to. I don't know what love is yet, I just know I'm feeling weird when I see him or talk to him and I've been thinking about him lately. I tell my friend EVERYTHING, but I don't know if I should tell her this.

Feeling Different Than Before

Dear F.D.T.B.,

You could drop a hint like, "Your brother is really nice." But next time you're all together, it might be awkward to know that your friend would be aware of how you're feeling. What does your gut say? Is this interest one-sided? Is he flattered by or oblivious to your attentions? If he likes you back, are you ready for things to escalate? If not, will you be able to hang out over there without blushing? Whatever happens, keep making time for your best friend.

Dear Carol,

I have a crush on my best friend's brother. When I told my best friend, she told her brother who told his friends who told their friends. Now everyone knows! God, I hate being an eighth-grader!

Not So Secret Crush

Dear Not So,

It's not a crime to have a crush, so don't die of embarrassment. The question is: Has he been acting different? Smiling extra? (Hurray!) Ignoring you? (Darn, but at least you know not to waste more time pining over him.)

Dear Carol,

My "friend" is going out with my brother and ever since, she has been calling me every day and asking for him. They talk for hours and she never asks to talk to me! I am feeling left out because I got them together. Should I confront her?

Left Out

Dear Left Out,
Why not? Say, "I'm glad for you both but I miss you, too." You can also tell your brother how you feel—in person or in a note.

Dear Carol,
One night at my house we were playing flashlight tag. My cousin and I were hiding with this boy I liked. I asked her to ask him if he liked me. They hid so she could ask him but then she told me he didn't like me. And then they started going out! I feel like beating the crap out of my cousin. What should I do?

Feel Like Smashing

Dear F.L.S.,
There's not much you can do, but don't pummel her. You two will be cousins forever and those two will probably break up in a blink. Hang in there and either forgive her or argue it out and then try to forgive her.

Dear Carol,
I told my friend what guy I like and the next day she said, "When you mentioned it, I decided I like him, too." She drives me crazy!

Who Gets The Guy?

Dear Who,
Depends who The Guy likes. Can you two make a pact that if one of you starts going with him, you won't flaunt it in front of the other and you'll both try to keep getting along?

Dear Carol,
I like this guy on my bus. So does one of my friends. I may be dreaming, but I think he kind of likes me. He sits next to me and leans over my seat and stuff. So now I feel awful because I'm supposed to be listening for my friend to see if he talks about her, but he talks to me a lot. He's gone from being a cute jerk to a hot sweetheart. My friend said that if I ever went out with him, she would never talk to me.

Torn

Dear Torn,
Yours is a sticky, though not uncommon, situation. I don't think people can really call dibs on a crush. If (and only if) things heat up with the guy, you may have to come clean to your friend. Say, "Look, I have to confess that I like him, too." If she talks about canceling your friendship, remind her that you didn't break them up, you just have similar tastes, and you're sorry and you value her friendship. Will this be easy for her to hear? No. So if things take off, try not to gloat (or glow!) in front of her.

Dear Carol,
I'm neighbors with a boy my friend likes. I like him,
too. My friend got up the nerve to tell him that she
likes him, but I didn't. Now they're going out and I'm
jealous. When she comes over, all she talks about is
him and how perfect they are together. If I talk about
something else, she'll interrupt and ask if we can go
over to his house. How can I get her not to do that
without hurting her feelings?

Needs Advice

Dear Needs,
She doesn't seem to be worrying about hurting
your feelings, so speak your mind. Say, "I'm
happy for you but I feel jealous and left out
when you talk about him. Let's talk about other
stuff." Or simply, "Did you come over to see me
or him?"

Dear Carol,
There's this boy in my class I have a MAJOR crush on.
But he's already got a girlfriend and I already have a
boyfriend. He's all that I think about and the bad
part is ... his girlfriend is my best friend in the whole
entire world!

Found My Man

Dear Found,
Yipes! How would you feel if tables were turned—
if she were coming on strong to your main

squeeze? It will be easier on your friendship if their relationship dissolves on its own rather than getting deflated by you. Keep your hands in your pockets. At some point you and he will probably get a chance to get together, but why do it now when it might devastate your best friend? Are you really willing to sacrifice one relationship for another?

Dear Carol,
I am totally in love with my best friend's boyfriend and I think he likes me, too. My best friend doesn't go to our school anymore. I know you are going to say that boys come and go and best friends are once in a lifetime. But I really like him.

After Her Boyfriend

Dear After Her Boyfriend,
I would indeed say that if she were still at your school. Since she has moved and long-distance relationships can be fickle, I may cut you a little slack. Girls often fall for friends' guys because those guys have been "preapproved" and because the girls have had a chance to get to know them. Before you step up the flirting, ask yourself if there isn't someone else you could like. Even if their romance is coming to a natural end, if you take her place at his side (and she finds out), your friendship with her will be at risk. Stakes are high, so tread carefully!

Dear Carol,
I'm going out with this kid who's kind of overweight.
I really like him and he's sweet, nice, and funny, but
everyone keeps coming up to me and saying, "You're
going out with him? Isn't he, ya know, FAT?" I hate it
when people diss him.

Fatty's Girl

Dear F.G.,
It sounds as though your boyfriend is nice and
your friends are rude. Be true to your own feelings. People have different tastes and one girl's
hottie is another's ho-hum. Since being fat isn't
ideal for health, if your boyfriend himself is
uneasy about his weight, suggest taking a walk or
riding bikes together. Maybe you can be a good
girlfriend and a good influence.

Boyfriend Problems

Dear Carol,
So I finally have my first boyfriend. But my female
friend is best friends with him. They talk and do more
stuff together than my boyfriend and I do. Sometimes
I think they have strong feelings for each other.
Should I back off and see if their friendship could be
more?

Clueless In Love

Dear C.I.L.,
Don't roll over and play dead unless you wouldn't mind if your boyfriend becomes an ex-boyfriend. If you would mind, make more of an effort to talk in person (or on the phone or on-line) and plan fun activities with him.

Dear Carol,
I think my best friend is trying to steal my boy-friend. She tells me he cheats on me and she calls him a lot. I don't want to lose my best friend or boyfriend.

Fallen In Love

Dear Fallen,
Your friend isn't being very friendly. Assuming your boyfriend cares about you, can he think of anyone who might like to go out with her (so she can leave you two alone)? Tell your friend that it bothers you that she calls your guy so much and that you'd appreciate it if she backed off a little.

Dear Carol,
I don't like some of my boyfriend's friends. Also, his old girlfriend used to be my friend, but now she hates me. So does my old boyfriend. I wish I could be still be friends with both of them, and not with my boy-friend's friends.

Messed Up

Dear M.U.,
And I wish I could make the best-seller list! It is hard to stay friends with exes and boyfriend's exes, but it's possible and with a little civility, you can move past the hatred. While you probably should act friendly to your guy's friends, you don't have to give up your friends for his. If you *dislike* his friends, ask yourself why he hangs out with them—or why you hang out with him.

Dear Carol,
I am going out with this guy but he wants to keep us a secret. I don't want to. He says he doesn't want to ruin his reputation with his popular friends. He's afraid of people making fun of him.
                                              Top Secret

Dear T.S.,
I'm not impressed with your boyfriend's reasoning. If he cares about you, he can tell his popular friends how terrific you are instead of acting ashamed of you. If he doesn't care about you, why go out with him?

Dear Carol,
I have started going out with a boy who I have liked for a year and a half. He is taking up a lot more time than I expected. My friends are mad at me because I spend more time with him. I love my friends like sisters and I hate it when anyone gets mad at me.
                                        Trouble In Paradise

Dear Trouble In Paradise,

Never mind your friends and boyfriend, how do you feel? Are you enjoying your boyfriend, or would less time be more fun? Your friends may be jealous, or they may have a point. Figure out a better balance of friends, boyfriend, family, homework. There is never enough time for everyone and everything, but maybe you and your boyfriend can get together less often, but still talk on the phone or on-line. His friends and family might also appreciate knowing that he has some afternoons for them. You don't have to devote all your time to each other just because you're going out. And if someday you do break up, you'll want your friends to be there for you—but they may not be if you don't pay attention to them now.

Dear Carol,

My boyfriend is really sweet but he doesn't do anything. We've been going out for several months but he is shy and I'm the one who asks him to dances, movies, the roller rink, or anything like that. My best friend's boyfriend does all of that plus gives her gifts for no reason and requests songs on the radio. Should I dump him?

Why Have A Boyfriend?

Dear Why?,

Some boys are more attentive, romantic, and talkative than others. You can break up if your romance isn't all that fun. Or you can accept your shy guy as is. Or you can say, "I usually invite you out and I'd love it if you would invite me out." Or you can get him talking with open-ended questions like, "What's your all-time favorite movie?" Or "What were you for Halloween when you were little?" Or "What are your grandparents like?" Or "Do you remember your dreams?" If you give your boyfriend a present (anything from a CD to a candy bar), he may reciprocate. But you know what? The feelings you exchange count more than the gifties.

Dear Carol,
My boyfriend gets mad because I chat with boys
on-line.

Chatterbox

Dear Chatterbox,
One terrific boyfriend is worth several cyber-buddies. His jealousy is natural and shows he cares. How would you feel if he had lots of on-line female friends? Reassure him that you like talking with him the most (if that's true) and spare him the details of your cyberchats. Remember, too, that if a boy gives his age on-line, he may be years younger—or older. And (yup, I know you know this, but) never give out your real name or address.

Dear Carol,
My boyfriend doesn't say "I love you" on the phone

even though I kissed him. I tell him I love him.

Love Or No Love

Dear Love Or No Love,
Saying "I love you" is a big deal. If he acts like he cares and thinks you're great, that also speaks volumes. Try not to pressure him into labeling feelings before he's ready. In my time, I've kissed a number of guys, but said "I love you" to only a few!

Dear Carol,
I have a boyfriend, and I call him a lot. When we hang up, I want to say "Love ya," but I'm scared he'll say, "What?" On-line we just say "cya" or "g2g" (see you or got to go).

First-Time Lover

Dear First-Time Lover,
Fear can be good. The fear that is holding you back is helping you not to rush this romance. If this relationship is meant to last, there will be plenty of opportunities to express your love. If not, you'll be glad you listened to the inner voice telling you to wait. On-line, you could also consider signing off XOX.

Dear Carol,
My boyfriend often tells me he loves me, and I think I might love him, but somehow I can't get myself to say it back.

In Love Or Not

Dear In Love Or Not,
Some people declare love at the drop of a dime; some confuse love and lust; and some might feel loving but be reluctant to say so. Don't force yourself to name your feelings. But do tell your boyfriend that you care about him and have never liked a guy as much as you like him (or whatever). If you think he's eager to hear those three little words, you can even admit that you can't say them yet but that he's your #1. When you're ready, with him or someone else, the words will come.

Dear Carol,
Help! My boyfriend invited me to the Junior Prom, but I don't know how to dance.

Left Feet

Dear Left Feet,
Most couples don't know precisely how to waltz, mambo, jitterbug, fox trot, or do each step of the dance-of-the-moment. But all you really need to know is how to hold each other (not too tightly, not too tentatively). And you *can* do that! If your boyfriend is a dancing-school graduate or has great rhythm, tell him you're up for some pre-prom practice. For faster dances, just move your shoulders, hips, arms, and legs in a fluid and creative way. Imitate the style of friends you admire. Finally, relax, because the other dancers won't be focused on you anyway—they'll be concerned

with how they look and what their partners are thinking. Here's a dancing tip from the late great Fred Astaire: "I just put my feet in the air and move them around."

Dear Carol,
I have a boyfriend and we make a great couple. But he has a used-to-be best friend who is always flirting with me. I don't like him, and he is making my boyfriend mad. I feel like I'm being forced to break up with my boyfriend and go out with his friend.

Cupid's Victim

Dear C.V.,
You're not. No one is using force, so decide not to be intimidated. It's possible that the flirt feels left out because the guy he used to spend time with now spends time with you. Can you discuss this with your boyfriend? You might even encourage them to talk about what's going on or to go do something fun together.

Dear Carol,
Yesterday I went with my friends to the mall. One of my best friends, a boy, gave me a present. I was amazed and I gave him a hug. At that moment I saw my boyfriend behind us. For some reason, my boyfriend was offended. All I did was give my best friend a harmless little hug. My boyfriend will not talk to me. He just ignores me.

Harmless

Dear Harmless,
Your boyfriend may be blowing things out of proportion, but it's not fair for you to act 100 percent innocent and indignant. I can see why he feels threatened by that hug, can't you? Maybe your romance has run its course, and you aren't that interested in his feelings anymore. That happens. But if do you want to keep going out, be honest with your boyfriend and yourself. You, too, might feel a twinge of jealousy if your boyfriend's best friend were a girl and you saw them exchange a gift and a hug.

Dear Carol,
There is this new boy in my school. We've been going out and at first it was great. He was my first kiss and my second and third and at least a dozen more. But now he's suffocating me. In school when he walks me to classes, I feel like shouting GET AWAY FROM ME! But on weekends I miss him so much and I want to talk to him and hang out with him.
What's A Girl To Do?

Dear What's A Girl To Do?,
Hmmm . . . You don't want to break up with him, but you do want some breathing room. That's reasonable, but hard to express delicately. Try. Take a deep breath and tell him how much you like being with him but that you need more time in school to hang out with girlfriends, too.

Dear Carol,
I just moved to a new state. On the first day of school, I met a cute boy. I really like him, but I told my old boyfriend I'd call him every day. When I told my boyfriend about the boy, we got in a wicked fight. When he asked why I told him, I said because I always tell him everything.

Messed Up

Dear M.U.,
Sounds like you and your old boyfriend had an honest relationship. But at your age, it doesn't necessarily make sense to swear loyalty and put your love life on hold until you get to see him again. If you live hours apart and are attracted to someone local, it may be time to close one chapter and start another. Of course, a breakup will feel bittersweet, especially since your old boyfriend might start dating others, too. But if you handle all this with care, perhaps you can stay friends, have fond memories, or even go out in the future. (Say, "I'll never forget you, but I think we're too young and far apart to keep going out," not "You're history because the guys here are way hotter!")

Dear Carol,
I've been going out with this cute guy for two months. The problem is that my mom doesn't know that. I tried to ask her if I could have a boyfriend, but she said, "We'll talk later." But we don't talk. My

*boyfriend gives me a lot of things, and my mom asks,
"Who gave these to you?" and I say, "My friend." But
I don't like saying that because my mother and I have
a good relationship.*

Help!

Dear Help!,
If you told your mom about your boyfriend,
would she flip out or be OK with it? You could
keep your secret, but since you are tempted to
tell, consider saying something like, "Mom, I've
been wanting to tell you that I'm sort of going
out with this boy and he's really considerate, and
things aren't moving too fast and we're not going
anywhere or doing anything you would disapprove of." At your own risk, of course!

*Dear Carol,
My boyfriend never calls. Whenever I tell him to call,
he tells me to answer the phone because he thinks my
parents hate him. They don't. If my dad answers the
phone, my boyfriend hangs up. So now he doesn't even
have the guts to call anymore. What should I tell him?*

Call Me

Dear Call Me,
Tell him that you understand his feeling self-
conscious but that when your dad answers, he
should say, "Hello Mr. ——, this is ——. May I
please speak with ——?" Tell him if he goes the
polite route, your parents will be impressed.

Dear Carol,

I am going out with a great guy with a lot of good qualities and he likes me, too. But he lives on a farm so his father sometimes kills their animals to eat, and sometimes my boyfriend and his father go hunting. This goes against everything I believe in since I'm vegetarian and won't even wear leather. How should I deal?

In Love (With Animals)

Dear In Love (With Animals),
If you're looking for a reason to break up, you've got one, ready-made. But if you two are going strong, keep going out. You'll never find a guy who is A-to-Z perfect for you, and maybe this person is close enough—for now anyway. When it comes to actual marriage, it's important that couples have values that are as compatible as possible. For now, consult your head and heart and decide whether you're in or out.

Dear Carol,

I'll be 16 next month. What I want to know is how can you tell if a guy really loves you? I've been going out with a guy for almost four years. We've broken up a few times but we always get back together. I really love him a lot, and he tells me he loves me, but sometimes he acts like he doesn't care. Like not calling me or not coming over when he says he will. That makes me mad and sometimes I tell him I want to break up, but then he asks me to go back with him and of

-232-

course I do, because I'm miserable without him. Is
this really love, or is he using me just to have a girl-
friend? When I get upset over him, my mom always
asks me why I love him so much and I just tell her the
truth: "I don't know."

Love Questions

Dear Love Questions,
Love questions rarely have easy answers. But
keep asking yourself why you love him. You two
started going out when you were almost 12, and
I bet you and he have both changed a lot. Is your
relationship a habit? Or do you really enjoy talking with him, doing things with him, hugging
him, hearing about his troubles, and telling him
about yours? Some of the initial excitement may
have faded, but if you don't feel warm and happy
with him and you can't count on him, there's
no reason to give the romance more and more
years. You say you are miserable without your
boyfriend, but after the lonely pain of breaking
up, you might meet someone with whom you'd
have more wonderful times. It's your decision
whether to improve your relationship or set each
other free. But his being your first serious boyfriend doesn't mean he is the only match for you.

Dear Carol,
OK, here is my awful situation. This summer I went to
Greece for three weeks. I met someone very special
and we fell in love. We spent every possible moment

together until I had to come back to America. I've been home now for a month, and he is all I think about. Everything I do, see, say, and hear reminds me of him. At night I lie awake thinking about all the good times we had and then I start to cry. I love him so much it is driving me crazy.

Help!

Dear Help!,
You had an idyllic summer. Don't go having an awful school year because of it. If you can visit him or he can visit you again, that would be great. Meantime you can write or perhaps e-mail each other. But do your best to get into higher gear here at home—audition for the school play, join the lacrosse team, get on the yearbook committee. First love is heady stuff, but believe it or not, you *can* feel this way again, perhaps for someone in your own hometown. You enjoyed your summer romance, but there are other seasons ahead. He was your first love, not your last.

Breaking Up

Dear Carol,
I just dumped my boyfriend for three good reasons. #1. I don't want to date just one guy. I want to have lots of fun with lots of guys and I'm not ready for a big relationship yet. #2. He is such a crybaby! Every

time we would get into a fight, he would cry like it was the end of the world. I like my guys strong, not that sensitive. #3. He treats my friends terribly. He told one of my friends she was annoying right to her face.

Did I Do The Right Thing?

P.S. Here is a poem for my ex-boyfriend:

**Roses are red,
Violets are blue,
Trash is dumped,
And so are you.**

Dear D.I.D.T.R.T.?,
It's fine to break up with someone, not fine to be mean about it. He's hurting. Don't make things worse by circulating your poem or bad-mouthing him.

Dear Carol,
My boyfriend is kind of weird and he doesn't call me anymore except when he wants money. My friends and family say to dump him but I can't, it's too hard. What would you do if you were in my shoes?

Don't Know What To Do

Dear D.K.W.T.D.,
Dump him—civilly. He was your first boyfriend, not your last, and I hope the next one talks with you instead of using you as a bank. You could say (or write a note that says), "I feel too young to be

committed to one person, so I think we should break up." Or just un-stick yourself quietly from this guy because you deserve better.

Dear Carol,
I have a really sweet boyfriend and a great relation-ship. It's as close to perfect as it gets. He buys me a rose often, but not too often. We hug and kiss and are totally into each other. Only one problem. I don't seem to be interested anymore. I don't know why either. He's so sweet. I can't hurt him by breaking up.
Not Interested

Dear Not Interested,
If you're feeling ho-hum, you aren't as totally into him as you say and things aren't as perfect as they may have been. Old Married Couples sometimes go through stages of waxing and waning passion yet hang in there because they are a good match or because they have kids or both. But if your romance has gone stale, there's no reason to do couples therapy or stay together through thick and thin. Most middle-school relationships aren't meant to go the distance. Since he's giving you flowers but not making your heart sing, move on and let him move on. Will he be bummed to hear that the show's over? Yes. But he'll bounce back as will you.

Dear Carol,
I have a boyfriend who likes me a lot. My parents

love him. But I've been noticing other guys, and I don't like him anymore. How do I tell him without breaking his heart? I kind of want to play the field.

Boyfriend Blues

Dear Boyfriend Blues,
Lots of devoted girlfriends notice other guys, so that alone would not spell trouble. (Cute guys can be eye candy. What's not to notice?) But if you don't like your boyfriend anymore, it's time to bail. You're the one cuddling up with him, not your parents. Say something like, "I don't want to hurt you because I care about you, but I don't really want to keep going out. I think we're too young to be tied down. I'm sorry." Or "My feelings have changed," or "I hope we can be friends." How you break up matters, so go easy and don't upset him right before his finals or a big game. And don't be seen immediately holding someone else's hand.

Dear Carol,
Every time I call my boyfriend, he doesn't want to talk. When I write him letters, he throws them away. What's up with him?

Ignored By Boyfriend

Dear Ignored,
What's up with you? Why are you shortchanging yourself? He is not giving you the time of day, so don't give him any more of your time. It sounds

as if he broke up with you and forgot to let you know. (Not very nice.) I'm sorry if my reply seems blunt, but your so-called "boyfriend" is a thorn in your side, and as soon as you take that thorn out and flick it away, you'll feel a lot better. You'll also feel freer to get to know other—nicer—guys.

Dear Carol,

I was going out with this boy. While we were going out, he told my friend that he wanted to break up with me and go out with her. I was sad and mad! Finally, I broke up with him. Now I'm wishing I hadn't. I still like him a lot. I also think I don't want to go out with another boy as long as I live because I'm afraid he'll do the same thing.

Missing Him

Dear M.H.,
Ouch. You may wish you hadn't broken up with your ex, but what else could you have done? Tied him to a chair? You miss him, and he hurt you, but it's not fun to go out with someone who doesn't want to go out with you, so you were right to let him go. Take your time before sharing your heart again, but don't swear off the male of the species just because this guy acted like a gerbil. Don't give him that power in your life. You're still a great person, and if you get out there, you'll meet someone terrific who appreciates you. (P.S. I'm assuming your so-called friend was

telling you the truth. It is, of course, always best to try to talk directly with a boy rather than to have some outside person pronounce your relationship dead or alive. Remember how garbled messages got when you used to play Telephone?

Dear Carol,
I have a best friend that's a guy and a best friend that's a girl. They used to go out, but they broke up, and now I'm falling for my best friend that's a guy. I told my friend that's a girl, and she said she would hate me because it's like having her leftovers.

Boy Versus Bud

Dear Boy Versus Bud,
I don't see anything wrong with having someone's leftovers (if they are yummy), but I can see why your confession upset your friend. If you leave things alone, your male and female friendships will be safe. But if you and he are finding each other irresistible, proceed with caution, and just do your best to spare your friend the mushy details of your romance. Will she feel jealous? Maybe. She's human.

Dear Carol,
My boyfriend and I just broke up. Right after that, he asked my best friend out. They both know I'm sad, but they don't really care. I feel that I can't talk to either one of them.

Sad And Betrayed

Dear Sad And Betrayed,
That stinks! You don't have to pretend that you're happy for them or that this isn't tough on you. You're in a lousy situation, and if you weren't feeling sad right now, you'd be a Martian, not an Earthling. Hang out with other girls and guys and figure out what you can add to your life—a sport, hobby, activity, or weekend away at your cousin's. You'll feel better soon.

Dear Carol,
My boyfriend really likes me, but I don't like him that much anymore. Right when I was going to break it off, he said, "I'd be better off dead," and "I love you so much. If you ever dump me, I'll kill myself." I talked to my mom, and all she said was, "You're too young to even have a boyfriend."

Help!

Dear Help!
Wow. That's hard and it seems unfair, doesn't it? But when someone talks suicide, you can never take it lightly or assume the person is bluffing. I want you to be able to ease out of his life without setting him off. If you know and trust his mom, you might consider speaking to her about this. Or ask a favorite teacher or advisor. His survival is not your responsibility, but since we don't know how stable he is, when you do bow out, do so extra gingerly. Use "I" not "You" sentences, like "I care about you but I realize I can't handle such

a serious relationship," not "You're not as fun as you used to be." Can you subtly encourage him to talk to a counselor or clergyperson and to get more involved in group activities—band, theater, sports? Since he has threatened suicide, you might also tell him that you care about him but refuse to be emotionally blackmailed. Try to find a nearby adult to talk to about all this. Good luck.

Dear Carol,
I went out with this boy for two months and I cared about him deeply. Then he dumped me. I cried for three hours. Two weeks later, he asked me out again. I said yes because I still liked him. But he ended up dumping me again.
Trapped In A Love Bubble

Dear Trapped,
If you're still stuck in that love bubble, pop it! Your ex is not the only guy around and you're not a yo-yo on his string. I know you feel awful. But call three girls today to make plans. Get a jump on your next book report. Play pool or go bowling. Make cookies with your sister. Shoot hoops with a neighbor. Take tap. Most of all, don't give him another chance to hurt your heart. Let his wishy-washiness be his problem, not yours. Falling out of love (or like) can be harder than falling in, but you have better relationships ahead. He was not your one-and-only *grand amour*. (P.S. You know the oldie "I Will

Survive"? Learn the words and start belting it out in the shower.)

Dear Carol,
I have a really caring and cute boyfriend. We talk and take walks and we almost kissed. Now I'm about to go to a different school and I don't know if he'll want to stay together. I'm worried we'll break up and I don't want to. Should I ask him if he wants to break up or let it be?
                    In Heaven But Not For Long?

Dear In Heaven,
If you say, "Do you want to break up?" he might assume you do. Since you can talk, talk. Tell him you hope you'll keep going out even after you switch schools. He probably hopes the same thing. There's no guarantee you'll be a couple forever, but there's also no reason to say good-bye before you want to.

To Kiss or Not to Kiss

Dear Carol,
My boyfriend and I have been together for about one year. We used to just talk on the phone and chill together. Recently he's been more friendly. He always has his arm around me or holds my hand. Last week he gave me my first kiss! It was on the cheek. He kisses me on the cheek and on the nose a lot now (maybe once every hour)! Soon he'll be on my lips.

*I'm not ready for that. I don't know how to say no.
What should I do? I love him and I don't want to
break up.*

Too Fast

Dear T.F.,
Since you love him, be honest with him. Tell him
to slow down because all this kissing is making
you nervous. Talk it out—you'll probably feel
closer afterward. As for not knowing how to say
no . . . learn, because you're at an age where
peers may urge you to smoke or drink or take
things or do things you don't want to.

*Dear Carol,
My friend told me that she has kissed a boy. I like
a boy and I want to kiss him. My dad says you
have to be 16. I'm 12. How old do you think you have
to be?*

Kisser

Dear Kisser,
I don't think there's a right age. What matters is
if you're going out and care about each other and
can talk. You'll know when the moment is right.
Meantime, try to be patient—you're not behind!

*Dear Carol,
I've been with my boyfriend for five months. He's
ready for "French kissing." I guess I'm ready, too; but
I'm only 13. I don't feel any pressure, and he doesn't*

make a lot of moves. What should I do if we end up
alone?

Still A Beginner

Dear S.A.B.,
Since neither of you is rushing the other, take
your time before taking steps. You're not on a
schedule.

Dear Carol,
All the people in my fifth grade are going out—even
kissing. I think we are a little young. All my friends
do is talk about guys with cute butts. It gives me a
stomachache.

Confused About Guys

Dear Confused,
Maybe you aren't confused. Maybe they are. No
matter what they say, all the people in your grade
are *not* dating or kissing. As for conversation,
while boys' butts can be interesting, so can lots of
other subjects!

Dear Carol,
I am going to a party and I was warned we were
going to play Spin The Bottle. Could you please
explain step by step how to kiss and French kiss?

Virgin Kisser

Dear V.K.,
Step One. Put your face near his. Step Two. Tilt

your face so your noses don't collide. Step Three. Put your lips near his. Step Four. Close your eyes OR look into his eyes. Step Five. Close your lips OR part your lips slightly. Wait! Wait! Wait! Wait! Wait! Wait! What am I writing here? There are no rules or rights or wrongs to kissing—especially when you're kissing a guy you like who likes you (which, I'm afraid, is not always the case in a Spin The Bottle game).

Dear Carol,
My friends were playing Spin The Bottle and the bottle spun on the cutest guy in the eighth grade. I was so tempted but I was afraid my boyfriend would dump me if he found out. Well, my friends moved it up to Seven Minutes In Heaven. I went in the closet and he started kissing me and feeling my breasts. It hadn't even been one minute! Now I have the guilt of the year because the guy that I made out with was telling everybody in the school that I put the moves on him. What if my boyfriend finds out? He is so cute and sweet and I don't want to lose him.
Scared To Lose My Love

Dear S.T.L.M.L.,
I'm sorry the boy was a blabbermouth, and I hope that if your boyfriend finds out, he forgives you. But if he'd let his hands roam over some other girl's chest, you'd be hurt and angry, right? You can't really have it both ways. If your boyfriend wants to break up, and you don't, apologize

and tell him you made a huge mistake rather than trying to defend yourself or blaming it on Mr. Fast Hands. (And next time don't get carried away—no matter what your friends say. Or don't play a kissing game if you already have a boyfriend.)

Dear Carol,
I was really into this boy, and he wanted to French me. Well I finally agreed to. After I did, I found out he thought I tasted like crap (only he didn't say crap). Well now I'm scared to go out with guys because I don't want to get hurt. If he ever asks me again, should—never mind, I guess I know the answer to my own question.
Scared And Lonesome

Dear S. And L.,
What an immature low-down jerk! I'm sorry that happened. Don't give up on all boykind, but don't hurry to kiss someone you don't trust and care for either. His comment is a reflection on his beastliness, not on you or your breath. (Worried about halitosis? Brush your teeth more or use a mint before kissing!) If you ever do contemplate kissing *him* again, I think—never mind, you can guess what I think!

Dear Carol,
I have a boyfriend and I have a question. How do you

get rid of hickeys off your neck and does it give you
any disease? I don't want my parents to find out.

Hickeys

Dear Hickeys,
The good news: Hickeys don't give you a disease.
The bad news: You can't make them magically
disappear. You can hide them with a concealer or
foundation or under a turtleneck or scarf. But
next time your boyfriend puckers up, tell him
not to leave a souvenir of his passion!

Dear Carol,
I was supposed to have a private time with my
boyfriend at my house while my mom and dad were
out. My mom came home early and saw me and my
boyfriend making out on the couch. My shirt was
half-off. She threw him out and grounded me for one
year. I have been sneaking out to see him every night.
Should I tell?

Smooch Smooch Baby

Dear Smooch Smooch Baby,
If you tell, your mom will probably hit the roof
all over again. Is there a part of you that wants
to slow things down with the boyfriend and almost wishes she would ground you for real? It's
not easy to be your parents' baby and your boyfriend's baby, so think about what you really
want.

Dear Carol,
I'm 13 and all my friends are using drugs and losing their virginity to boys they hardly even know. I feel pressured to do that stuff, too, but I know it's wrong.
Missing The Kissing

Dear Missing The Kissing,
The overwhelming majority of 13-year-olds are virgins. That's a fact. But once one girl claims to have been-there-done-that, others pretend they have, too. You are right; being reckless is wrong. If your friends really are a fast-moving bunch, hang out with other kids. Every year about 10,000 girls 14 or under do become moms, and believe me, that's not ideal for the babies or the girls who cheat themselves out of childhood. It's hard to go to a movie, a dance, or college when you have a baby to care for. Being a parent is a big job. You know that, because you see how busy your parents are working, cooking, cleaning, shopping, paying bills, and leaning on you to make your bed and do your homework. For now, grow up at your own pace and stay far away from drugs. Someday, you will have a boyfriend and you won't be missing the kissing. But even then, I hope you'll know that sex can wait.

Family Matters

#####

At school, you may be feeling fine and looking good and talking with girls and guys. How about at home when no one's watching? Do you snarl at your sister, bark at your brother, fight with your father, and moan to your mother? I hope not! I hope you're making the best of your nest. After reading this chapter, you may even appreciate your family more than ever—and get along with them better, too.

My Parents Treat Me Like a Baby

Dear Carol,
My mom thinks I'm not ready to go to PG-13 movies,
but I'm sure I am. I already know about guy-girl stuff,

and I've heard all the bad words but I don't say them.
(Sometimes my parents say them!!)
Already Ready

Dear Already Ready,
Some movies stink, whether they are G, PG, PG-13,
or R. Others are terrific. Say, "Mom, let's go to the
video store and pick out a movie we can watch
together." Once there, find movies that have good
reviews right on the box. Consider starting with
Romeo and Juliet. Explain that it will help you
understand the language of Shakespeare (valid
point) even though anyone who would do what
they did for love is crazy (also true).

Dear Carol,
My parents treat me like a baby. My mom calls her-
self "Mommy" and my dad "Daddy." They are way
overprotective and want to know every detail of
my life. When I asked when I could start dating, my
mom said, "The traditional age is Sweet 16." Get real!
Wait, it gets worse. Some of my friends now assume
my parents won't let me meet them so they've
stopped inviting me places. I love my parents, but I
wish they'd loosen up. My mom is very sensitive so
I can't exactly talk about this.
Not A Baby

Dear Not A Baby,
You can try. Since you don't want to be treated

like a baby, approach your parents as maturely as possible (that means no yelling, accusing, whining, or crying) and tell them you love them and understand why they are protective but wish they'd recognize that you can handle a little independence. Sound rational, not emotional, and let them see how adult you are by keeping up your grades and by helping with dishes or trash or pets. Tell them that since you're in the double digits, you wish they would stop referring to themselves as "Mommy" and "Daddy." But don't argue over when to date unless some guy is already asking you out. (Why spend today fighting about tomorrow?) As for friends, invite them over and tell them to keep including you in. If you have an especially polite friend (you know, a real parent-pleaser), have her come over so your parents can see that peer pressure doesn't always spell trouble. Finally, recognize that your parents may trust you, and you may be trustworthy, but they're wise to be wary of the Big Bad World.

Dear Carol,
I try to tell my parents I'm growing up, but they won't listen. We are not very close. My parents just pretend we are a close family in front of other people. My mom always says if I don't listen to her, I'm not her daughter anymore.

Baby

Dear Baby,

Try, "Mom, I do listen to you, and I'll always be your daughter." Say it respectfully, and don't expect instant results. Is it possible that you have been acting like a little kid while hoping to be treated like an older kid? (Just asking!) You'll all be happier if you get along so keep working toward your common goal. (P.S. Most families behave better in public than in private.)

Dear Carol,

My parents invade my privacy. They barge into my room, listen in on my phone calls, read whatever is on my desk, open my mail, and go through my drawers. My brother got messed up with drugs, which is why they are overprotective, but I'm a good student and I haven't given them any reason to be suspicious. So it bugs me that they keep bugging me.

My Room Is Not A Garage Sale

Dear M.R.I.N.A.G.S.,

Your parents may think they are snooping for your own good, but enough already! Don't scream, "Leave me alone." Do remind them that you are a good kid who is not hiding anything, and that it hurts when they act like they don't trust you. Say that you understand their concerns, but you and your brother are separate individuals, and also that you'd never read their letters or walk into their room without knocking. (Right?) Can you be more open so they have less reason to be curious or worried? Instead of saying, "I'm going out," say, "I'm going to Lily's to do our science project." When you come home, instead of racing to your room, spend a minute saying hi to your parents. By the way, lots of girls have similar complaints, and if I were writing your parents instead of you, I'd tell them to give you a break!

Dear Carol,
My camp is planning an overnight trip to go white-water rafting. I was totally looking forward to it until I told my mom. She said that unless she was coming with me, I couldn't go. I know whitewater rafting isn't the safest thing to do, but I'm sure they wouldn't take us unless they knew what they were doing. I don't want to pass this up!

Adventure Deprived

Dear A.D.,
Without getting loud, ask what she's worried about. Is it the rafting? (You'll wear a life jacket . . .) Is it the overnight? (You'll be asleep by 12:00.) Is it the . . . ? Find out. Suggest she phone the camp director or a parent whose child went last year. Consider saying, "Fine—come along." (Not ideal, I agree!) And remind yourself that she's being protective because it's hard to let go.

Dear Carol,
I really want to get a second ear pierce or tattoo.

I think I should be able to since it's my own body, but my mom says no.

Not Fair

Dear N.F.,
It *is* your own body, but it started inside your mom's, and she's worked hard for years taking care of it, and I assume she's still buying most of the food that goes inside it and clothes that go outside it and providing the desk and bed where it hangs out. Which is why I think she still gets some say in what happens to it. Besides, lots of people who get holes and tattoos change their minds, so it's not the worst thing in the world to have to wait a little bit. Think about it? And think about how you can make a statement with clothes, jewelry, or hair, or even temporary tattoos.

Dear Carol,
For my 13th birthday, I want to have a boy-girl party. But I'm afraid to ask my mom because I think she'll say, "Those boys will start a game of Spin the Bottle."

Birthday Girl

Dear Birthday Girl,
If you don't ask your mom, you definitely won't be having a boy-girl party. So you may as well ask. If she freaks, drop the idea until next year. When you two are getting along, you can say, "Is it hard

watching me grow up?" or ask if she remembers how she felt at her first boy-girl party.

Dear Carol,
I want to go out with boys but how can I explain to my mom that what happens to some people doesn't happen to everyone? She's an investigator who has worked on too many cases with gangs, and she likes to watch **Unsolved Mysteries** *and* **America's Most Wanted**.

Smothering Mothering

Dear Smothering Mothering,
At least you can see where she's coming from. Plant a kiss on her cheek and tell her that you read that a parent's job is to give a kid roots and wings, and that you've got great roots but if you don't start testing your wings, you'll be all grown-up and still living at home. Say "I think your career is cool, but you don't want me to grow up paranoid, do you?"

Dear Carol,
My dad and I used to be close. But ever since I got a boyfriend, I've rebelled against him. When my dad wants his little hugs, I feel like I'll scream if he touches me. What's wrong with me? I know I'm so precious to him.

Overprotected

Dear Overprotected,
Consider the world from your dad's point of view. Yesterday you were little and huggable and happy to be his angel pie. Today you'd just as soon he back off to make room for Spike. That's called growing up, and it can cause growing pains for kids and parents. Your rebellion is understandable, but so is your dad's hurt, so try to be affectionate with words or hugs, at least occasionally.

My Parents Are Not Easy to Talk To

Dear Carol,
I need my mom to help me out but she won't. She never does anymore. She treats me like I'm 20 years old, but I'm not. Normally I'd like that, but sometimes I still need her, and she doesn't get it.
Not Twenty

Dear Not Twenty,
Let her know that while some kids complain about being overprotected, you'd welcome a little more mothering. If you express this kindly—not meanly—she'll at least listen, and listening is half of conversation. You might also suggest having lunch out, going for a morning or evening walk, shopping, getting a manicure together, signing up for a sketch class or self-defense course, seeing a play, movie, or ballet, visiting an out-of-town relative—just doing something fun together.

Dear Carol,
I have been going through lots of changes lately. I know I had my period but I am afraid to tell my mom because I'm the youngest and I'm afraid she won't treat me like she used to. I cry just thinking about what she'll say if I tell her.
Perplexed, Bewildered, Baffled, Mystified

Dear Perplexed, Bewildered, Baffled, Mystified,
Good vocabulary! Since you're already upset about what she might say, be brave—you may find that what she actually does say is not so bad. Even youngest kids are allowed to grow up, and she won't suddenly start treating you differently. Everyone has mixed and moody feelings about puberty, but just because you're becoming a woman doesn't mean you can't still enjoy being a girl. Besides, awkward conversation isn't much worse than awkward silence. If you level with your mom, she may congratulate you or hug you or ask if you have questions. Would it be easier to write a note? Try, "I feel stupid writing this, but I want to ask you about pads" (or whatever). Still unable to talk to your mom? Hmmm. Are some of those siblings sisters? Or can you speak to your aunt or grandmother about this?

Dear Carol,
I can never seem to talk to my mom about girl stuff. I tried buying her cards, but she only seems to be happy for a moment. I feel lonely and I'm jealous

*when my friends' moms take them to the movies,
malls, out to lunch, everything. I asked my mom if
just the two of us could spend time together. Well, it
didn't work because we got in a major fight. Please
help. I need my mom. At times I feel as if I hate her
when really I love her.*

Majorly Bummed Out By Mom

Dear Majorly Bummed Out By Mom,
I'm sorry your mom is letting herself miss the
pleasure of your company. About that fight . . .
what caused it? Did you say, "All my friends'
moms take them places and you never take me
anywhere!" or "All my friends' moms buy them
piles of clothes"? If so, consider, "Mom, I love you
and need you. Let's go out to lunch just us, OK?"
or "Thanks for the new backpack—I love it." Keep
trying to reach your mom. Ask about her relationships with her mom or best friend. Ask
which movie stars or musicians she thought were
cute—and don't laugh. Compliment her lip gloss
or new shirt. Heck, ask about her day. And next
time you are both losing it, remind yourself that
it takes two to fight. Then, instead of firing off
the last word, try saying, "I see your point" or
"Sorry" or go ahead and do the thing she's after
you about. (Try this—it works.) I'm sure your
mom would like to be closer to you, too, even if
she's not as aware of that as you. If she remains
unreachable, however, please know that you can
become close to a mentor, relative, or friend's

mom. And some dads are better at girl talk than some moms.

Dear Carol,
Please, I ask you, read this letter, take it seriously, and write back promptly. My mom is very very very very mean. Not strict, just mean. I always try to tell her that I'm tired of this, but she never takes it in. How would you feel if your mom never listened, was always in your business, never let you have big friend get-togethers, and was always complaining about you?

Mom-Be-Gone

Dear Mom-Be-Gone,
I'm sorry your mom is no fun. People who act mean are usually unhappy. I wonder if she feels that you don't listen to her or always complain about her. Break the pattern. Instead of saying that you're tired of her, roll up your sleeves, give yourself an invisible gold star, and give her a compliment as you help set the table or fold the laundry. Cut through her meanness with kindness. Even if it doesn't work, you can be proud of yourself for trying.

Dear Carol,
I don't love my dad. Is that strange? I wish my mom would divorce him. He is military-strict and never lets me do anything, not even watch TV. We never talk.

Father Hater

Dear Father Hater,

Look at things for one second from his point of view. Maybe he walks in after a hard day and no one jumps up and says hi or asks him anything. Maybe, just maybe, he's lonely and doesn't even realize it because his own kid tunes him out in favor of the boob tube. Can you pretend he's a friend's dad and that you're stuck having to make pleasant conversation? Say, "How was work?" or "Did you have a favorite pet when you were a kid?" Anything! He may be able to improve his attitude if you nudge him persistently. Can you ask your mom to give him some pointers? Of course it's also possible that things won't change much. If so, work on accepting this rather than hoping for change and being constantly disappointed. What a loss. Stay out of his way when he's angry and remind yourself that in a few years, you can be off to college.

Dear Carol,

My father is so retarded. He'll start saying "Cut it out" over and over in an annoying voice that is imitating me. He acts like a three-year-old and when I tell him to shut up, he tells me, "You shut up!" and then I say, "You shut up, you idiot," and we keep saying it until I finally get him to shut up.

On My Nerves

Dear O.M.N.,
You two are in a horrendous pattern of pushing each other's buttons and being incredibly rude and disrespectful. You'd both be happier if you'd stop acting as if it's your job to entertain a talk-show audience. Change won't be easy without a counselor (or even with one), but why not tell your father today that you want to try to set a new tone? You could even consider signing a contract stating that neither of you will say "Shut up" anymore—whoever does has to put a quarter in a penalty box. Time apart would probably help, too. I'm sorry your dad acts so juvenile, but unless you like the idea of your own children cursing *you* out someday, do start rising above his immature behavior rather than acting awful back. Then, instead of having the last word, you'll have the satisfaction of knowing that you are being an adult.

Dear Carol,
I found out that my dad was married before he married my mom. It upsets me because I found out accidentally. I feel like I'm being lied to. Should I confront him?
Sad And Confused

Dear Sad And Confused,
Although this news must have been a shock, I doubt your dad meant to lie to you. He may have

kept his past under wraps because he didn't want to upset you or didn't know when to bring it up. If you have a close relationship with him or your mom, consider asking about the divorce instead of sitting on the secret. Don't accuse them of a cover-up. Tell them that you are feeling sad and confused and listen to what they tell you.

Dear Carol,
My parents are divorced and I live with my mom and I see my dad on weekends. He smokes, and it really bothers me. When I go there I have to stay in my room because of the smoke.
Clogged With Smoke

Dear C.W.S.,
It's hard to change grown-ups. But make sure your dad knows that you're not avoiding him— you're avoiding his smoke. Say (or write) that smoke bothers you. If it's too hard for him to cut back, maybe you two can at least take walks outside together.

Dear Carol,
My dad is seriously taking a big jump into the unknown world of politics. He has a good heart but it's a big position and he's embarrassing our whole family. How do you nicely say, "Cut it out"?
Embarrassed

Dear Embarrassed,
Sometimes daughters feel like they're going to die of embarrassment when all their parents are doing is breathing in and out. I understand your feeling mortified because your dad is in the spotlight, but can you try to convert some of your discomfort into pride? Or can you shrug it off? Your dad isn't in the news because of being an ax murderer, after all. And your true friends won't ditch you any more than you would dump them if their parents became senators. As for talking to your dad, you probably can't say, "Cut it out." But you can ask that he not tell reporters any stories about you.

Dear Carol,
This is not a question; it's a story. My dad was depressed because he dumped his girlfriend. My brother and I go to my dad's every other weekend. Well, I put about 15 "I love you" "#1 Dad" "You're the greatest Dad" notes all over his house. He called me later saying he loved the notes. One of my dad's friends said he really needed the notes, and they made him cry. So I would just like to say that if you mess up with your parents or just feel like they need an "I love you," but you don't know how to come out and say it, these things really work.

Been There

Dear B.T.,
Glad to hear it! Thanks for writing.

My Parents Have Sky-high Expectations

Dear Carol,

I have taken piano lessons for more than three years. I was the one who wanted to take them, but now I want to quit. Both my mom and dad say I can't quit because I'm so good, and my mom wants me to be in something musical in school, but there's only choir and I don't want to be in choir. I also don't want a different piano teacher. Why should I be forced to do something hard and boring and expensive that I don't even like? Every time my mom asks me to practice, we argue or I end up crying. We've had long talks, but my parents just don't understand.

Piano Bummed

Dear Piano Bummed,
Some kids love piano; some don't. Maybe your parents are worried that you'll quit other things as soon as they get difficult. Write a note that says, "I'm not a quitter; I'm just not a pianist," and instead of saying how boring and hard piano is, say you've benefited from your lessons, but now you'd like to devote your practice time to learning a new skill or keeping up with schoolwork. Or compromise. Take piano every other week. Or think again about joining choir—maybe with a friend? Your voice is an instrument you can take with you anywhere.

Dear Carol,
All my parents care about is grades. They don't want
me to get Cs anymore. Last report card, I got a C in
math. I thought they were going to kill me. Whenever
I try to talk to them about how I feel, they yell at me.
My mom is not as bad as my dad. I know they care
about my education, but they hurt my feelings.
They're always overlooking the good points about
me just to talk about the bad points.
   Thinking About Putting Herself Up For Adoption

Dear T.A.P.H.U.F.A.,
Did you get a good grade and they forgot to praise
you? Say so. Tell them you want to hear when
they are proud, not just disappointed. And be
sure that you dish out compliments along with
complaints. Remind yourself that your parents
care about your education because they care
about you and your future. Math is hard? Can
they arrange for a tutor? Or can a high-school
student bring you up to speed without charging
too much? Ask your teacher or guidance counselor for a recommendation. It is hard to excel
under pressure. But without pressure, sometimes
it's hard to get things done. We all work harder
when something is due or a test is ahead. Can
you psych yourself up to move up a row in class,
stay organized, and find a quiet place to work at
home? As your grades go up, your parents will be
pleased, and so will you.

Dear Carol,
My mom is always making me try different sports and activities. Sometimes she signs me up for a sport or activity without even telling or asking me. Whenever I tell her that I don't like that sport, she pretends she doesn't hear me or tells me it'll help me lose weight or become healthier.

Needs Advice Quick

Dear Needs Advice Quick,
I agree with you that your mom should talk with you before signing you up for things. But I agree with her that sports and activities are good for you—body and soul. Sit down with her and figure out which appeal to you, and take it from there.

Dear Carol,
I need help with my dad. It seems we hardly go a day without fighting. I try to talk and be civil, but he won't listen. No matter how perfect I am, I'm not perfect enough.

Not Perfect Enough

Dear N.P.E.,
When parents act like ogres, it may have little to do with you. They may be tired or hungry, or things went poorly at work, or their own dads were mean. Don't give up on your dad. But don't transfer his dissatisfaction or impossible

standards onto yourself either. You're not perfect, but maybe you *are* perfect enough. (P.S. Any chance you can ask your mom to buy him a book on parenting? How would he react if you took one out of the library?)

Dear Carol,
Sometimes I feel like my parents expect too much and I have to do everything at once, you know, be a perfect daughter, super student, great athlete, good friend, and participate in lots of activities, and I get—

Totally Stressed Out

Dear Totally Stressed Out,
If it's your parents who expect too much, tell them you're feeling stretched too thin. They may love that you're a good person and an achiever, and may not realize how stressed you feel. You may find, however, that you're actually pushing yourself, not just getting pushed. For energetic people with lots of friends and interests, life can be exciting—and sometimes exhausting. Take care of yourself by getting enough sleep, downtime, and nourishment. Remind yourself that you want to enjoy life, not just live efficiently or squeeze everything in or do everything well. Remind yourself, too, that if you're anxious about the school play or cast party afterward, that is Positive Stress. Too many activities? Which can

you do without? No time to get together with friends? Touch base on the phone or on-line.

I also lose my balance from time to time because I want to do everything (throw parties! write novels! speak at schools! bake cookies! answer letters!). But when I start teetering, I tell myself to calm down and that there is time to do everything—just not all at once.

My Parents Are Hard on Me

Dear Carol,
My parents have started to blame my attitude and ideas on my being a teenager. They think I will be a bad-mouth bad-attitude teen even though I'm a good kid. They also tell everyone, "She's 13 now, so we better watch out!" Will I have to live with this for the next six years?

Frustrated

Dear Frustrated,
It sounds like they are preparing themselves for the worst. Maybe they were rebellious teens. Tell them that there is something called the self-fulfilling prophecy and that if they keep thinking you're going to turn rotten, you just might, but that you wish they'd stop announcing that you're about to have a personality transplant. (If

they keep it up, try to roll with the punches instead of taking it personally.)

Dear Carol,
This may sound silly, but I feel like my parents think everything is funny. They are always making fun of me and laughing. I try to talk to them but they laugh more, and once when I cried my mom called me a big baby.

On The Verge Of Tears

Dear O.T.V.O.T.,
Are they making fun of you or getting a kick out of you? There's jovial laughter and cruel laughter. Either way, they are bumming you out so try again to tell them how you feel. Or leave a note on their pillow. Something like: "Dear Mom and Dad, I love you but when you laugh, it makes me feel as though you don't take me seriously." Parents are hard to change, but when you look them in the eyes and make a reasonable request, they may at least understand your point of view. If their laughter keeps hurting, ask a relative or school counselor for help.

Dear Carol,
I constantly get picked on by . . . you will never guess . . . my parents! I am a little overweight and my father and my mother always call me Porky, Chubby, Fatso, Fat A**, and other names. Is it normal for

parents to call their children names?
                    Parents From The Black Lagoon

Dear P.F.T.B.L.,
I won't say it's not normal, but it sure isn't nice, and I'm sorry it's happening. Speak up! Ask them in person or in a note to call you by your name. If possible, enlist an aunt or grandparent to help you. Someday you will be old enough to choose to live with people who act considerate instead of cruel.

Dear Carol,
Out of curiosity, is calling your kid worthless, stupid, useless, dumb, etc., verbal abuse? Is it illegal? What are the consequences? What are some of the things parents do if they are abusive physically? Is hair-pulling punishment or abuse?
                        A Girl Who Needs New Parents

Dear A Girl Who Needs New Parents,
Some parents are less ideal than others and I'm sorry if yours are acting hateful instead of loving. Physically abused children sometimes have broken bones, bloodied faces, or dark bruises that can be photographed or used as court evidence against a parent. Broken hearts and battered spirits are harder to show or prove, yet verbal and emotional abuse are real and all too common. If a particular parent is big on hair-pulling and name-calling, it's hard to say whether he or she is breaking any

laws. But are there consequences? Yes, because kids need support just as plants need sunshine.

If you are putting up with being put down, and talking to your parents won't help, confide in a trusted adult friend, relative, clergyperson, or counselor. Can you move in with an aunt or grandparent, maybe for the summer? Take comfort in knowing that you won't be living at home forever. If you are or could become a stellar student, think about attending a boarding school, perhaps on scholarship or financial aid.

Dear Carol,

My parents hit me and chew me out. They want everything to be perfect but nothing is perfect unless you are God. Do I look like God? I don't want to tell my friends or teachers, but I do want them to stop hitting me.

Crybaby

Dear Crybaby,
You are not a crybaby, and I'd like to chew them out! Some parents fly off the handle and say or do things they later regret. Some kids try to understand or forgive them while also trying to live on tiptoe. If you get hit a lot and don't feel safe in your own home, think about talking to a trusted adult (a relative? school counselor? minister or rabbi?) or placing an anonymous call, maybe from a phone booth, to ask for information or

help. Talk to the Child Abuse Hot Line at (800) 422-4453, or the National Domestic Violence Hot Line at (800) 799-SAFE, or call the Covenant House nine-line at (800) 999-9999. You are not alone, and a nearby adult can help you, but you may have to ask for that help. Keep believing and protecting yourself. Things can get better.

Dear Carol,
I'm so embarrassed that my mom still spanks me over her knee. Normally, she grounds me, but a couple of times a year, she loses it and I get a hand spanking on the bare bottom. My mom says she got spanked until she turned fourteen, but that was the old days. Am I the only one? My girlfriends might laugh if I ask them about their punishments.

Age Thirteen

Dear A.T.,
I'm sure you're not the only one, but I wouldn't rush to ask your friends. I'm against spanking children, and spanking teenagers definitely seems inappropriate. Try not to set your mom off, but if you do, tell her to dock your allowance, ground you, give you more chores, or whatever, but that you're a young woman now, and spanking does not seem right.

Dear Carol,
I overheard my mom talking to my grandmom (her mom) on the phone. She said, "I don't know how I

could raise a child so different from me," and then "She is such a ditz." I don't have any sisters so I know she was talking about me. I don't want to confront her.

Talked About

Dear Talked About,
That must have hurt, but I'm sure you've said less-than-complimentary things about people you love, too. (Probably even your beloved mom?) Try to let it go. If the snippet you overheard keeps bothering you, tell your mom. Apologize for accidentally eavesdropping, and I hope she'll apologize, too—or maybe even explain that Grandmom has asked her, "Have you heard about Lulu?"

Dear Carol,
I hate both my parents. I mean, I just can't stand them. They are so mean to me and each other. I want them to get a divorce. I want to move out of this house and away from them. My mom keeps saying, "Go ahead, leave." But I don't know where to go. I'm only 11 and I've hated them for about three years and I feel like if I don't leave, I'll go insane.

(Almost) Insane

Dear (Almost) Insane,
The ideal would be for your whole family to get some counseling. But if your parents won't agree or say they can't afford it, you (yes, you!) can still talk to a professional to work out some of this anger. As for running away, girls who just get

on a bus often wind up with far worse troubles since they can get picked up by people who want to take advantage of them and who use drugs or have diseases. It's better to take a step in the right direction than to run in the wrong one.

How can you find a counselor? Ask your school guidance counselor, pediatrician, or family doctor for a referral. Sessions can be secret. They can even be free if your school, church, or synagogue has the facilities or if your parents have excellent insurance. If you have a friend who has talked to a therapist or counselor she liked, get his or her number.

My Parents Fight a Lot

Dear Carol,
My parents yell at each other a lot. I hate it. I've asked them to stop, but they haven't. Is there anything I can do to make them?
Seriously Stressed

Dear S.S.,
Probably not. Try to stay out of it and try not to take sides. Their problems are not your fault and keeping the peace is not your job. Some parents have loud marriages but deep down get along fine just as some siblings always bicker but still love each other.

Dear Carol,
When my parents fight, my temper goes up. We moved and where we used to live, I could take a walk and go to a little pond and sit in silence and watch the fish swim. Now I can't do that anymore.

Out Of Place

Dear Out Of Place,
I'm sorry your parents are butting horns. The move was probably stressful for everybody. The pond, however, sounds lovely, and you know what? It's still yours. You may still be able to go there and feel some serenity just by closing your eyes. Try it. Can you see the fish swimming? Or can you find a new special place?

Dear Carol,
I can't have friends over because my dad swears all the time and my parents argue constantly. One time, my friend called twice in a row while I wasn't home and my dad screamed at her. I know my friends talk about it behind my back. I go to their houses, and they are probably wondering why I never invite them over.

Why Me?

Dear Why Me?,
What a shame. You're not alone, of course, and I'm glad you have friends whose families welcome you over. Since you suspect your friends are already talking, be frank. Say, "I'd invite you

over, but it can get pretty loud at my house." Though friends may feel for you, I doubt they hold that against you. If you do decide to invite a friend over, warn her that your parents can be gruff, and if things get out of hand, go outside. (P.S. Your friends' parents fight, too.)

Dear Carol,
Every time my parents fight, I lock myself in the bathroom. Pathetic, huh? Sometimes when I'm asleep they fight and it wakes me up. My dad always talks about my mom's side of the family in a bad way. How can I make them stop?
Helpless

Dear Helpless,
Unfortunately, kids can't make parents stop fighting any more than parents can get sisters and brothers to call a truce once and for all. In a calm moment, you can remind your dad that when he criticizes his in-laws, he's dissing your relatives and that hurts. You can also tell your parents that you love them but hate when they act like enemies. Meantime, I don't blame you for hiding in the bathroom. If you have music in your bedroom, you could also turn up the volume or hole up with headphones.

Dear Carol,
Today my dad was talking about leaving my mom if some things kept happening. I have friends whose

parents have gotten divorced, and it doesn't look the least bit fun. Is there anything I can do?

Parent Trouble

Dear P.T.,
You can say, "I love you both and I hope you can work things out." You can even suggest marriage counseling. But your parents are adults and are going to do what they feel they must. They will not, however, fall out of love with you. While divorce is definitely not fun, for some kids it works out better in the long run than living with parents who stay together despite rage, scorn, or indifference.

Dear Carol,
About two hours ago, my dad left, and he said he needed time to think about stuff including if he still wants to be married. He said he'd be gone for a month. He didn't say why or where he was going. I'm not like other kids—I don't think it's my fault. I think it's my dad's fault, and I'm mad at him for leaving. Do you think my parents are getting divorced and do you have any ideas why he left?

Sad And Mad At Dad

Dear Sad And Mad At Dad,
I'm really sorry you're going through this. Don't assume the worst yet. Maybe your dad will come back today or tonight or long before the end of the month. Do I know why he left? No. Marriages can

falter when men and women fall out of love with each other or fall in love with different people or argue nonstop about money or . . . lots of reasons, and it's rarely just one person's fault. You and your mom both need extra love right now, so be gentle with each other. And if your dad calls, don't just blast him. Tell him you miss him and, if it's true, that you hope he's coming back. His side of the story probably differs from your mom's.

Dear Carol,
My parents are fighting and talking about getting a divorce. What if they get one? What will happen to me?
Scared

Dear Scared,
Don't jump to conclusions yet. Fights are scary, but your parents may just be letting off steam. Even if your parents break up, they'd still love you, and you would not be left out in the cold. You'd probably end up living mostly with one parent but spending time (weekends? vacations?) with the other. Sometimes parents make the arrangements; sometimes kids choose whom they want to live with; and sometimes judges pick the parent they think would do a better job caring for the children.

Dear Carol,
My parents keep getting into fights and when I am invited to my friend's house, I never go because I

*am afraid that my parents will get divorced and I'll
have to choose who to live with.*

Saving My Family

Dear S.M.F.,
Staying home will not save your parents' marriage any more than going out will sabotage it.
After all, they could decide to call it quits while
you're at school or asleep, right? Please do everything you can to keep your own life full and
happy. If your parents ever do split up, it won't
be because of you, and you would need your
friends.

*Dear Carol,
My parents are divorced and every time they are
together, my mom trashes my dad. I'm afraid to even
let them talk on the phone. Some awful things happened between them, and my mom always threatens
to send a sheriff after my dad.*

Torn

Dear Torn,
How terrible! Your parents once loved each
other, and now they act as if they hate each other.
Remind yourself that they love you. And see if
you can find (or start) a peer group at school,
church, or a community center where kids with
divorced parents can talk about their complicated feelings.

Dear Carol,
Right now my family is really low on money and my
parents are fighting. What can I do?

Feuding Parents

Dear F.P.,
Not much, though this would not be a good time
to tell them that you long for everything you
see in commercials or that your friends get
allowances or are planning trips. It's hard for
kids to make money, but if you are motivated and
responsible and have your parents' permission,
it's not impossible. You're great with children?
Place a notice about baby-sitting in a nearby
school or pediatrician's office or in your building lobby if you live in an apartment. You're
patient and smart? Tell grade-school teachers
that you can tutor younger kids in math or reading. Got a green thumb? Weed gardens, mow
lawns, rake leaves, and shovel driveways. Get the
word out that you're willing to walk dogs, feed
cats, or run errands, and you may soon be able to
pay for more things yourself. As for your parents'
fights, slink away from the line of fire.

Missing a Parent

Dear Carol,
My parents are divorced. My dad moved to another
state. My mom won't let me spend the whole summer

with my stepfamily and real dad—only half the sum-
mer. I want to be with them the whole summer.

Sad Because I Want To See Dad

Dear Sad,
Divorce is rough on kids! Is your mom reluctant
to let you go because she'd miss you or because
she's mad at your dad or doesn't trust him? Who
has legal custody during the summer? If you can
find out, it may help you determine what to do.
Explain to your mom that you miss your dad.
Since your father moved away, she may be afraid
to let you go away, too. Reassure her that you love
her tons and will send letters or e-mail and be
back before she knows it. I hope you can be sensitive to your mom's feelings and ultimately stay
close to both your parents.

Dear Carol,
My dad ran away when I was 3. He got married and
has other kids. I miss him. I'm afraid to call him. I
asked him to visit once and he said no. I was won-
dering if you can get Oprah Winfrey to reunite us. I
also want to ask my mom about him, but I don't want
to bring back painful memories for her.

Dadless

Dear Dadless,
I'm so sorry your father has not been there for
you. While it's tempting to idolize your dad and
dream about a TV reunion, it's important (though

painful) to recognize that he has a new life and hasn't been responsible or loving in yours for years. Try to accept his absence and focus on the adults who care about you now. By hoping for your father to change, you may be making it harder for yourself to move on. As for talking to your mom, you're entitled to ask about your dad. But do so in a quiet moment when she has time to talk. Maybe a car ride? Say, "This is an awkward subject, but I've been curious about . . ." Who knows? She may be expecting you to say ". . . sex" and be relieved that you're asking about your roots!

Dear Carol,
I live with my dad. I haven't seen my mom in two years. She really wants me to live with her, according to her letters. She always sends me and my younger sister great stuff. I would like to see her again, but I'm kind of afraid. I have a right to be because she always hit me on the face, never fed me, and talked to thin air.
Tug Of War

Dear Tug Of War,
What does your dad think? How about your grandparents? It sounds as though your mom was unable to take care of you. Is she now taking care of herself? Was she sick and is she better? Or was she and is she still an unstable and difficult person? You're wise to be cautious, and while I hope you can continue communicating with her,

and perhaps even see her, there's no reason to pack up and move.

Dear Carol,
My parents are divorced. I feel like it's my fault. My mom's in jail. I'm really sad. I'm trapped in my own little world. I miss my mom. I'm scared that my dad will take me away from my mom. I want to see her. Help me get out of my world.

Trapped

Dear Trapped,
I'm sorry your life is so upside down right now. Things will NOT always seem this bleak. Your parents' divorce is not your fault, but of course it is hard on you, as is having a parent in jail. Are you trapped? No. But it will take effort to climb out of the hole you are in. How are things at school? Is there a teacher or principal or counselor who listens to you? Is there a librarian who can point you toward helpful books and community programs? Is there a subject or activity you excel at that you can do more of? Do you have a caring relative to talk to? Ask your dad about seeing your mom, and ask why she's in jail. He may be worried that it won't be good for you to visit her, but maybe you can tell him that though you don't approve of whatever she did, she's still your mom and you still love her. Take care of yourself and work hard so that you can get out of your little world by joining the bigger one.

Dear Carol,
My mom had a boyfriend and he was like a dad to me because he had taken care of me since I was two. Now my mom has broken up with him. I still love him a lot. Can I get them back together somehow, and if not, how do I still get to see him?

Minus One

Dear Minus One,
I don't think you can get them back together. But I understand that you wish this man was not out of your life just because he's out of your mom's. Talk to your mom about her feelings and yours. Work on a note explaining that you love her first and foremost and you don't want to upset her because you know this is a hard time, but that he was like a dad to you and you're hoping to talk to him and would she mind if you called or dropped a card or something? Sometimes kids and a parent's ex manage to stay close. More often, the party's over for everybody. Right now, he may miss you, too; so if you make it clear you want to keep in touch for your own sake, and not to get them back together, there's a chance your mom will approve. Of course it's also possible that she never wants to see him again, let alone trust him with her precious daughter. In that case, hang in there and please know that there will be other adults whom you will care about and who will care about you.

Dear Carol,
My mom has practically moved in with a man. She hardly ever calls or comes to see us. I love her, but I'm beginning to think I love my grandmother more. We live at Grandma's house.

Granddaughter

Dear Granddaughter,
It wouldn't be a crime to love your grandma more. I'm sorry your mom isn't always there for you— and I'm glad your grandmother is. Maybe she can help you arrange to see your mom more. Or maybe she can help you accept what you cannot change.

Dear Carol,
My dad hasn't talked to me for over a year. I've written him a million letters, but I've thrown them all out because they are either too nice or too mean. What should I do?

Hurt

Dear Hurt,
Write him one more. Start it: "Dear Dad, I've written you a million letters but I've thrown them all out because they are either too nice or too mean." Then finish it and mail it.

Dear Carol,
I live with my mom and sisters. I haven't seen my dad in two years. On the phone he keeps saying he will

come visit, but he never does. I miss him so much.
When he says he's coming soon, I don't want to say,
"You always say that." What should I say?

Waiting

Dear Waiting,
Love can be painful. Saying, "You always say that," would put him on the defensive, so tell him you miss him and are disappointed since it's been so long. Listen to what he says. You may also want to ask yourself (or your mom or a grandparent) what is going on. Two years is a long time.

Dear Carol,
I'm adopted. My body has been changing a lot lately and I've been wondering more about my birth mother—what she looks like and why she gave me up. My friend who is also adopted says she isn't curious about her birth parents because the parents who are raising her are her real parents. I love my parents, too, but I would like to find out about my birth parents. Any ideas?

Adopted

Dear Adopted,
It's natural to wonder about birth parents—and it's OK not to. Can you talk to your mom? She may feel threatened by your questions, so start with how much you love her and explain that

lately you've been wondering about your birth mother—whether she was big or flat, what she was like as a teenager, and what her circumstances were. Tell her you're not looking for parents (you have parents!), but for answers, and that you're curious—not unhappy. Your mother may be able to provide facts if she knows them or may be able to return to the agency that has your records. You may also be able to write a letter to your birth mother and include questions as well as your interest in hearing from her. Laws about privacy vary and when you're older, you may have greater legal access to your adoption files. Some adoptees find information on-line about domestic or international adoptions. For now, I hope your mom will be able to understand your curiosity about your birth mother, and that you will be able to understand any mixed feelings your questions stir up. Please know, too, that your birth mother may not welcome a reunion, and that if this is the case, that could be painful for you, but it would not be a reflection on you. Finally, the end of your search could lead to a beginning, because it's also possible that you and your birth mother could meet and even establish some sort of give-and-take relationship. What would you be hoping for? What would be hard for you? Support groups and post adoption services can help people sort through all this.

Feeling Forgotten

Dear Carol,
My dad gets on the Internet every night. That is all he talks about. How could I ask him nicely (so he won't be mad) to get off for a couple nights a week? I feel empty and I need love.

Off-Line

Dear Off,

It hurts to feel overlooked. Tape a note to his computer that says something like: "I miss you and would love to hang out with you one evening this week. Let's go to a movie, play a game, or take a walk. What's better—tonight, tomorrow, or the next night?" Add a couple of hearts, and I bet he'll come around. You could also e-mail him. Something short and sweet like, "Hi Dad! Here's a @—>—. Now go give your daughter a hug! :)" (When he hugs you, ask if he understood the rose and smiley signs.) You could also challenge him to a computer game. If necessary, enlist your mom's help to set up a weekly father-daughter activity: making pancakes on Sunday or bowling on Saturday. You'd be doing your dad a favor if you can get him to look away from his computer and toward his growing daughter.

Dear Carol,
We are moving and I had a 102 fever. I was waiting in my room for my dad, but he never came because he

was too busy negotiating on the phone with realtors. That's not all. For my first softball game, my dad promised he'd be there but he was an hour late because he said the people who wanted to buy our house wanted to bring their kids to see it.

Needs Some Attention

Dear N.S.A.,

It's nice that you want to spend time with your dad. But cut the man a little slack. Most dads aren't absolute villains or heroes. Your dad was trying to sell your house. As excuses go to be on the phone or be late, his wasn't bad. Many parents don't attend games at all. Talk to your dad, but be sure to give him credit along with the demerits.

Dear Carol,

I live with my mom. Ever since my dad got a girlfriend, I feel left out. I feel we compete for my dad's attention. When they kiss, it drives me crazy. And whenever my dad and I talk privately, she butts in and interrupts. My dad doesn't seem to mind. I am afraid to phone because what if she answers? Once we went out for dinner, and I asked my dad, "Can I sit next to you?" and he said I better ask his girlfriend. What's next? I feel like I don't belong. Is it wrong to feel this way?

Rejected

Dear R.,

Your feelings are your feelings. They aren't right or wrong. And I can see why you're frustrated.

Call your dad and if she answers, don't hang up or ask, "Is Dad there?" Say "Hi, how's it going?" then ask for your dad. Maybe he can give you undivided attention on the phone (especially if you have a question and not just a complaint). Tell him you would like to take a walk with him alone on Saturday. Tell him to put it in his appointment book. And say, "I love you, Dad, and I don't like feeling as though your girlfriend and I are competing for you. I bet there's enough of you to go around."

Dear Carol,
Ever since my mom got remarried, she pays all of her attention to my stepdad, and is always mad at my brothers and me for no reason. I wish my mom would take some extra strength Midol, and I'm starting to want to live with my dad.

Lousy Life

Dear L.L.,
This is a tricky time, but things can get easier. First, talk to your mom. Don't yell or accuse. Talk. Tell her you miss her and would love to spend a little time with just her. Say that you understand that she and your stepdad need adult time, then add, "but I wish we could do something to help us feel more like a family." Come up with ideas with her. A hike? Five-hundred-piece puzzle? Miniature golf? Sunday night popcorn and a video? Can you and your stepdad get along better? What

do you like (not dislike) about him? Living with your dad may be a possibility; find out. But for now, telling your mom you miss her (not that you resent her husband) is the first step toward harmony.

Dear Carol,
My mom likes this guy. I'm very uncomfortable with it. He always comes over and calls and I feel so alone. My life is ruined. You're the only one I can turn to.
                                                                    Scared

Dear Scared,
It can be hard to watch your mom be in love, but it's not necessarily terrible that a man she likes likes her back. Can you write her a note that says, "I'm happy for you but sad for me because I love you, too, and I miss you"? Can you get busier right now with friends and activities? Your mom may be dazed and distracted, but she's not abandoning you. Remind yourself that if you were in love, you would want your mom to understand if your boyfriend called a lot.

Dear Carol,
It seems that my mom doesn't love me as much as she used to. Like, she gives me a bunch of chores and yells at me when I talk back when all I'm doing is standing up for myself. Sometimes I feel like I'm not needed on Earth.
                                                                Not Needed

Dear N.N.,
You are needed and loved and occasionally taken for granted. Parents, too, are needed and loved and occasionally taken for granted. You're also getting older, which can mean more chores, less cuddling. But getting older can also mean more interesting conversations and games (Scrabble instead of Trouble, Hearts instead of War). Write a note to your mom and communicate your love, not just your frustration. To feel more needed, find out about volunteering in your community—reading to kids, planting a garden, helping a church feed the homeless.

Dear Carol,
I have a slight problem. My mom tells me she hates me.

Unloved

Dear Unloved,
Thoreau said, "Those whom we can love, we can hate; to others, we are indifferent." You probably couldn't care less about the shoe salesperson. But your family? You can love 'em and hate 'em. You are lovable, and your mom loves you, but I'm sorry she is not more careful with her words. If she ever says, "I hate you" again, don't say "I hate you back," say, "Well, Mom, I love you." You might even be the adult, and say, "I know lots of moms and daughters fight during these years,

but let's keep trying to get along." Last thought: If you have grandparents or relatives who think you hung the moon, hang out with them.

Dear Carol,
My mom is pregnant. Every time I hear her talking to my aunt, she talks about her and the baby. It makes me feel left out. I tried talking to her, and she said, "You know you'll be there." I think sometimes she doesn't love me.

Feeling Left Out

Dear F.L.O.,
Ten points for trying to talk to your mom. Your feelings are natural and when the baby first arrives, you may be even more jealous because of all the hoopla and gifts (not that you've been sitting around hoping for yellow booties or a duck mobile). Talk to your mom or aunt again and ask your mom to plan a special Saturday with you before the baby comes. Your mom probably would not be having another baby if she didn't love being your mom.

Dear Carol,
My sister and I swim competitively. At dinner each night my dad boasts about her times and her strokes. They hardly say a word to me. It's like I don't exist.

Nonexistent

Dear Nonexistent,
So start existing. Say, "I feel invisible," (not "You guys ignore me"). Say, "Let's play Pictionary or Boggle," (not "You love her more"). Tell them how your day was without waiting for them to ask. Ask about their day. Or put a note on their pillow or on-line that says that you get jealous when everyone praises your sister. By the way, is swimming your favorite sport? If so, great. If not, let your sister get wet while you excel at something else.

Dear Carol,
My parents decided to get an exchange student for a year. I thought, sure, why not, I've always wanted a sister. Well, she's driving me nuts! She skips class and doesn't do chores, and for some odd reason, they don't care. It's been over a month and they always talk to her and take her places. They don't even buy me a pack of gum. I wish she'd go back to Venezuela.
Neglected

Dear Neglected,
The girl in your house is miles from home, and your parents are trying to make her feel welcome. Even though you and she didn't immediately hit it off, you'll both feel better if you find some common ground. Can she help you with Spanish? Can you cook a South American dish together? Can you plan to visit her country someday? Soon she'll be gone whereas you will

always be the #1 Daughter. Tell your parents that you recognize that she may miss her parents, but that you miss yours! Say it sweetly, not nastily, and I can almost guarantee results. (P.S. I was an exchange student myself twice—can you tell?)

More Parent Problems

Dear Carol,
The worst thing ever happened the other night. I couldn't sleep, so I went downstairs to get some milk. As I was opening the fridge, I saw a man on the sofa kissing my mom. My mom is single so I know it's legal. Still, isn't she too old for that?

Confused

Dear Confused,
Nope. No one is too old to date or kiss or fall in love. Seeing them was a shock, but their embrace may not have been "the worst thing ever." Sometimes when a mom is feeling happy, that happiness can spill onto everybody. Consider saying, "Mom, I saw you kissing that man. What's he like?" Don't act horrified, and you two may be able to talk about it.

Dear Carol,
I have not been kind to my mom lately. Mean words slip out. What should I do?

Guilty

Dear Guilty,

If you realize you have been unfair to your mom, give her a hug or a handmade card and say that you're sorry you've been crabby. Then next time you're ticked off, think "I" sentences. Instead of saying, "You're always busy," say, "I miss you when I don't get to see you." Instead of screaming, "You're always telling me what to do," say, "I wish I could make some decisions." Start treating each other with more respect, and you'll both enjoy a more grown-up relationship.

Dear Carol,

My parents took away my dog and didn't tell me so when I went outside to play with him, he wasn't there. They also took away my cat. I took great care of both of them. I'm scared to talk to them about it because they will get mad, really mad.

Really Scared

Dear R.S.,

Whaaatt?? Are your parents monsters, or is there more to this story? Maybe your brother has allergies? You're moving overseas? The animals were ill? Your parents can't afford pet food? You're entitled to know what's going on, so pick a moment that is not hectic and ask whichever parent is easier to talk to. If you don't yell at them, they may not yell at you.

Dear Carol,
I have family problems, and I cause them most of the time. I think my parents want to send me to a doctor to talk about this. I don't know if I can face them again. I feel so rotten and scared.

Ashamed

Dear Ashamed,
They don't want to send you to jail; they want to give you the opportunity to talk out your troubles. That's not so bad. In fact it can be great to have a helpful listener. Lots of people talk to counselors, so put away the shame and open up to the doctor. You can start unraveling knots and stop bad habits your whole family may have gotten into. Maybe your parents can accompany you to a session or two.

Dear Carol,
My parents have been divorced for a long time. I stay with my mom, but visit my dad. My parents said that when I'm 12, I have to choose who I want to live with. My mom is OK for me. (I say OK because she is mean to me and nice to me.) My dad is wonderful to me. He treats me and my little brother to a lot of things. Can you give me some advice on which parent I should live with?

Which?

Dear Which?,

I can't tell you whom to live with. I can tell you that it's easier to act wonderful and generous when you're a part-time rather than full-time parent. In other words, if your mom takes care of you day-to-day, she's probably always saying, "Hurry up! You'll be late for school!" and "Did you finish your homework?" and "Brush your teeth!" Those may not be your favorite sentences, but they're more nice than mean. Do you have to make this decision or can things continue the way they are? Are there stepsiblings or stepparents involved? Would you have to leave your school? How does your brother feel? Your two parents? When you're sad or confused, which parent is best at making you feel better? Ask yourself if someone (a godparent? teacher?) who knows your parents can consider pros and cons with you. Your decision is important so it shouldn't be taken lightly, and I hope you'll manage to stay close to both parents, wherever you live.

Dear Carol,
My mom and dad are divorced, and my mom is dating this guy. I don't like him much. My mom usually doesn't let men smoke in the house because my brother is allergic to smoke and has asthma. But lately my mom's boyfriend has been smoking in the house and my brother has been using his inhaler a lot.

Angry And Confused

Dear A. And C.,

Lots of kids feel allergic to their mom's boy-friends, but since your brother really is, some-thing has to change. It's time for you or your brother to speak to her or her boyfriend. Politely but firmly. It may be as simple as saying to him or writing a note that says, "Because my brother has asthma, could you smoke outside instead of inside? Thank you very much—from him and me."

Dear Carol,
My number one goal in life is to get rid of my step-mother/stepmonster. She's an alcoholic and a smoker. Whenever she drinks, she starts lecturing me about boys and how to handle my life. She doesn't know how much I hate her. Neither does my dad. My mom does, though, and she tried to get me into Alateen. The only class I could get into had these rowdy boys that needed to be returned to their natural habitat, so I stopped going.
The "I Hate —— Club" President

Dear Prez,

I'm sorry you hate your stepmother and are sub-jected to her drunken tirades. Since it would be hard to change her, keep your distance and try to change your attitude toward her. Can you muster up some compassion along with the hatred? Let's also get you a more positive goal. Can you aim to be great at something? To fill a portfolio with sketches? To excel at cheerleading? To be a math whiz? To be more organized? To read a book a week? Some one-on-one time with your dad would also be a worthy goal.

Dear Carol,
My best friend is always putting down my step-father because we don't like him. I don't know what to do.

Confused

Dear Confused,
Explain that you want to vent but don't really want her to agree. Tell her that you're always willing to listen to her vent, too.

Dear Carol,
My parents are divorced. I see my dad every other weekend. When I come home and my mom asks if I had a good time, I'm afraid that if I say I had a really really good time, I might hurt her feelings. It's the same with my dad. If I tell him I had a great time with my mom, I'm afraid he might feel bad.

Stuck In The Middle

Dear Stuck,
Without going into great detail, tell them what you told me: that you don't want to hurt anybody's feelings, but the good news is, you enjoy being with both your parents. I hope they will be happy for you.

Dear Carol,
Last year I found out my dad was my stepdad. I've never met my real dad. Now my mom and dad (step) are having marriage problems and I'm really confused.
Mixed Feelings

Dear Mixed,
That's quite a bombshell. It sounds as though your dad (step) has been a real dad all along. I hope you can learn more about your biological father but can still stay close to the parents you are living with. I also hope they smooth things out with each other.

Dear Carol,
One day I was looking for a book in my dad's filing cabinets. I saw a bunch of magazines so I was nosy and checked them out. There were a few **Playboys** *and* **Sports Illustrated** *swimsuit issues. I don't want to tell my mom because I'm afraid she'll get upset and my dad will get mad at me if I give him away.*
Not Sure

Dear Not Sure,
Then keep the discovery to yourself. If your mom doesn't know, why tell her? And if she does know, she might not mind or she might not mind too much. If he kept a real woman stashed in his office, that would be a different story! (P.S. Your father is not the only guy with such a collection.)

Dear Carol,
My best friend got caught smoking and shoplifting in the past year. We have talked about it and I know she has changed. However, my mom still doesn't trust her. She won't let us go anywhere together. I really miss my friend.

Down And Out

Dear Down And Out,
I can see your mom's point and yours, too. Try, "Mom, I understand your concerns, but please give her another chance. She was acting stupid and she realizes it now. May I invite her over for the afternoon? I miss her." Your mom still says no? See your friend in school.

Dear Carol,
I made a new friend who is also my locker partner. We see movies, have sleepovers, and do other stuff best friends do. The problem is my whole family dislikes her. I can see why because when I'm around her, I act bad and different and sometimes I don't listen to my parents.

True Friend?

Dear T.F.?,
Why do you act bad and different? Wouldn't she like you for your real self? If she's getting you to curse—or worse—your parents may decide to stop welcoming her to your home, and you will both lose out.

Dear Carol,
I've had this problem ever since I was a baby. I can't
leave my parents. When they go out to walk the dog
or something, I think they will never come back. How
can I get over this fear?

Separation Anxiety

Dear S.A.,

I wonder why you feel uncomfortable when your parents aren't in view? Do you have a friend whose parents divorced or died? Did you get lost as a toddler? Do you feel you never get enough attention unless your parents are right next to you? There's a difference between separation anxiety and separation-anxiety disorder. If you just get jittery, take a deep breath and know that lots of kids find it hard to come out from beneath parents' wings. If you think you have the disorder (you can hardly go to school or to a friend's), talk to a professional, whether a school counselor or someone your doctor recommends.

Dear Carol,
My mom cut her hair. It used to be really long, but
now it's shorter than it's ever been. She asked me
what I thought and I just smiled and shook my head.
When I was real little, I used to use her hair as a
blanket and suck my thumb. When I got older, when
she hugged me, her hair used to come down and
drop on my shoulders. I loved that. It was as if I was
shielded by my mom's beautiful hair. I'm not very

happy that she cut her hair, but I don't want to in-
sult her.

                              Too Sad To Be Mad

Dear T.S.T.B.M.,
You were sweet not to insult your mom, though I'm sure she could tell from your smile that you preferred her hair long. (You can read her smiles, right?) Maybe your mom was ready for a change and has no idea that to you it feels like the end of an era. By the way, I found your letter poignant. Are you a future writer?

Dear Carol,
My mom is copying me. She dyed her hair blond like mine and uses my CD player. She is a great mother and all my friends think she could be my sister. That is not a problem, but I don't want her copying me!!!

                              Mom's Not Blond

Dear M.N.B.,
Having a glamorous mom can have drawbacks, especially if she wants to hog the limelight. But there's room for two beautiful women in one family. You aren't rivals. And since you may not be able to convince her to stop dyeing her hair, I hope you can convince yourself to feel flattered instead of threatened. The fact is: You're young, and she wishes she were.

Fearing and Facing the Loss of a Parent

Dear Carol,
My dad has brain cancer, and I think he's going to die.
He's seeing things such as animals dancing. I can't
take it much longer. During gym, I broke out crying.

Town Crier

Dear T.C.,
What a heartbreaking letter. I hope your dad
recovers. And I hope you can be gentle with yourself, especially if things take a turn for the worse.
Forgive yourself for crying in gym or anywhere
anytime. What daughter wouldn't? Right now, tell
your dad you love him. Write a note. Draw a picture. Hug him. And hug your mom extra, too.

Dear Carol,
My mom had breast cancer a few years ago and
sometimes I hear her crying at night. It scares me, and
I can't talk to anyone about it. I can't talk to my mom
either because she'll probably start crying again.

Scared

Dear Scared,
You obviously love your mom and she's obviously going through a rough time. I think you
can tell your dad or grandparents that you're
scared. And I think you can tell your mom you

love her and worry about her—or love her and hope she's going to be OK, whichever feels right. If it's too hard to talk, write a note. But don't just feel sad in your room while she feels sad in hers. Crying together is better than suffering alone. Please know that having breast cancer does not mean dying from breast cancer. When breast cancer is detected and treated early, survival rates are very very high.

Dear Carol,
I have a BIG problem. My mom died about a year ago and now I always worry about my dad. And I mean WORRY. I always think he's going to die somehow. It's getting so bad I don't even want him to go to the store without me. I don't even want to go to sleep at night because I fear he might stop breathing. Horrible thoughts flash through my mind. I don't think my dad can afford counseling. My friends think I'm a big wuss. Please help! You're my last hope.
Worried To Death

Dear Worried,
I'm so sad for you and you are not a big wuss. You'll always miss your mom, but talk to your dad about what happened to *her* and not just what could happen to *him*. In other words, your dad is fine. Healthy. A OK. You two are alive. So you need to act alive, to play and study and eat and sleep and see friends and get out of the

house. You need to reconnect with the here and now. Mourn your mom's death but recognize that she wouldn't want you to spend your days sad and worried. She'd want you to be vibrant and full of life and to do things that make you proud. Your fears are understandable. But they are crippling. Therapy would be ideal so ask your dad to try to find someone who is not too expensive, maybe a counselor associated with your school or a hospital, outreach program, church, or synagogue. Who else misses your mother? Her sister? Mother? Cousin? Best friend? Call them. They might welcome the opportunity to share memories and offer support. No one will ever replace your mother, but I'm hoping you can find an adult woman (a neighbor, friend, relative) who can be there for you during these years. In time your dad may fall in love again. If he does, the stepmother might also become a real mother to you.

Dear Carol,
About four years ago, my mom took me into her room and I knew something was wrong because my brother was crying very badly and then my mom told me that my dad had died. I was in shock. I could barely move. Then I burst out with tears. Now that I am older, I have been more sad than regularly because I see fathers everywhere. Will this pain ever stop?
                    Older And Sadder

Dear Older And Sadder,

Sometimes after a death, everyone does a very good and very important job of surviving—of holding it together and plodding through the days and weeks. Later, when the numbness and denial wear off and the enormousness of the loss sets in, people start feeling worse before they begin to feel better. I don't think you ever really get "over" the death of a parent. But you get through it, and after a while, you come to a point where you can finally remember good times with fondness instead of sorrow. While the pain may not go away completely, you learn to manage it. You know there's a hole, but you step around it, and you accept that the ache you feel is a tribute to the bond you shared. Time doesn't heal but it helps. By the way, those who have suffered are sometimes deeper and more sensitive than those who haven't. I'd rather have my father than my compassion, but the grief I endured when my dad died helped me to understand others who were grieving. I wish you still had your father, and I wish you'd had him longer. You'll probably hate Father's Day for a few more years. (I know I did!) But you will find love and comfort in the family and friends you do have. And you will feel better.

Dear Carol,
I read Girltalk and if I reopen old wounds, I'm terribly sorry, but I want to sympathize with you about

your father's death. I'd like to ask you a question. Have you ever had any dreams about your dad and felt his presence?

Wondering

Dear Wondering,
Thank you for your letter. I do sometimes have dreams about my father. In one, he told me where to get all the ingredients for *choucroute garnie*—one of his signature dishes. In another, he just sat quietly in an armchair at a family gathering. In another, he phoned and I was over-joyed to talk to him. Last week, my mother told me about a dream she had just had. "I dreamed that your brothers and you and I were going on a trip around the world—with different detours—and at the end, we were all going to meet Dad." Suddenly my mother looked up at me with tears in her eyes and said, "Maybe that's how it is." Maybe.

Big Sister Blues

Dear Carol,
This is long, so get ready. When I was 7, I was an only child. I was very lonely. Then my parents decided to have another child. I was so excited. The next year my parents decided to have another baby. So now I have two siblings. Four years later, they're such a drag. My things disappear, and I find them in my

sister's pretend purse or under my brother's bed. When I'm in school, they go in my room and mess things up. They also take my seat on the sofa and sing my favorite songs at the top of their lungs.

Siblings Are A Pain

Dear Pained,
Siblings can be annoying, but yours will grow out of the wild-child phase, and they copy you because they think you're cool. Can you ask your parents to keep them out of your room when you're away? A lock or door latch would help. Can you keep stuff in a drawer or on an out-of-reach shelf? Your sibs will soon be in school, too. And someday if you have children of your own, guess who the aunts and uncles will be? Since you're in each other's lives forever, make it for better instead of for worse.

Dear Carol,
I have to share my room with my younger sister and brother and I hate it. They borrow my stuff and I get no sleep and have no privacy. I WANT MY OWN ROOM. My parents say I shouldn't hope we'll move because we won't. This puts me in exasperation!

Stuck With Sibs

Dear Stuck,
Sharing a room is hard. Your parents may wish that they could give you each your own space but may be unable to afford such luxury. Can you

label some shelves and drawers for your stuff, some for theirs? Can you set some rules with your siblings—no borrowing without asking, and lights out at a certain time? Can you put up a curtain or sheet to divide your room? Can you all come up with more ideas?

Dear Carol,
I have a little sister who is afraid of the dark so she sneaks into my room and crawls into bed with me. I'm tired of it! My doctor said when it becomes a problem, to make her sleep in her bed. Well, it became a problem!

Sick Of Sister

Dear Sick Of Sister,
Being adored isn't always easy! Sometimes when a family problem bothers you more than it bothers others, you're the one who needs to brainstorm with your parents to try to solve it. Talk with your mom or dad when the night crawler isn't around. Calmly say that you understand their concern for your sister, but you'd like them to consider your feelings, too. Suggest they put a night-light or dimmer in your sister's room. Or that they put a sticker on your sister's calendar each time she stays in her own bed, then reward her with prizes for every three stickers (or whatever). You might also consider letting her sleep in a sleeping bag on your floor. This phase will pass!

Dear Carol,
My little brother is three months old. Whenever he starts crying, my dad starts telling my mom what to do and sometimes even yells at her. She ends up crying, which makes me cry.

New Baby Problems

Dear N.B.P.,
When there's a new baby, there's joy and chaos, and nobody gets enough sleep. Babies are delightful but demanding. Next time your parents act like children, offer to help hold the baby. Or just offer sympathy. Or ask, "Was I that loud when I was little?" and give your mom a kiss. The baby will soon be old enough to laugh and that may make you all laugh, too.

Dear Carol,
My mother expects me to take my brother everywhere. It's not fair. He's only three and he's cute and all, but why should I invite him to tag along with my friends?

Sister Not Sitter

Dear Sister Not Sitter,
If you tell your mother how you feel (without moaning), she may recognize that you're entitled to some private time with friends. Say that you love your brother and are willing to baby-sit a little but that with friends, he doesn't fit in. Make a deal that before or after you spend an afternoon

with friends, you'll spend some time (half an hour? more?) reading to or playing with him.

Dear Carol,
I have a younger brother who I watch like a hawk. My mom says he has to grow up and learn on his own, but I'm so scared for his safety. Am I wrong to be so protective?
                                                    Watchful

Dear Watchful,
He's lucky to have such a caring big sister. But toddlers do learn by walking, falling, and yes, conking themselves. Unless you think your mom is negligent or your brother is frail, try to ease up. Can you be protective without being overprotective? Matches are not OK; monkey bars are.

Dear Carol,
My mom was really smart in school. I'm a good student, too, but my brother who is younger is smart in a different way. She puts a lot of pressure on him. I try to stand up for him, but she says, "School is everything."
                                        School Isn't Everything

Dear S.I.E.,
School isn't everything. Feeling confident and happy and having friends and finding your strengths and being in activities and sports . . . this counts, too. Of course, being a good student

can help you feel confident and happy. Your brother is fortunate that you stand up for him. Maybe you can also tutor him—from you it may feel like a helping hand, not pressure.

Dear Carol,
My only sister is ten and is the crybaby of the family. She is overweight, does adequate in school, and appears to be talented in singing, which I can do, too. I am an excellent student, play the piano with talent, am a "social bumblebee" (my friend's phrase), and am slim. My sister always says "I hate you!" instead of "I love you!" I get angry at her, but then I feel bad, and I still love her. My problem: my sister. Cure her and I'm cured. How can I help as I always seem to enrage her? Sometimes I want to . . . you don't want to know!

Aggravated

Dear Aggravated,
Try to think of her as your teammate, not your rival. I'm sure she loves you, too, though she may not go around announcing it. Most siblings say "I hate you" more than "I love you." You two may never be close, but if you want to encourage rather than enrage her, start saying, "You sang that really well," or "You look good in that," or something positive. Your support will help her accept herself. Since you've been blessed with talents and graces, be generous. (By the way, your own mixed feelings are natural. Don't expect yourself to be a

saint and it will be easier to accept that yes, you love her, and yes, she can drive you bonkers.)

Little Sister Blues

Dear Carol,
I am the youngest of four. My older sister says I was a mistake, and my dad plays along. It really hurts.

Unloved Shadow

Dear U.S.,
Ouch! It's bad enough your sister is playing hardball, worse when a parent joins in. Do your sister and dad know how much this hurts? Have separate heart-to-hearts with them and tell them how you feel. Unfortunately some siblings and parents are hurtful, abusive, and not easily changed. If that's the case (I hope not!), then work on letting their barbs bounce off you and on feeling good and whole despite them. Other peers and adults love you for who you are (whether you were "planned" or a happy surprise!), so don't let a mean-mouthed sister trip you up.

Dear Carol,
My sister has her first real boyfriend. All she does is talk on the phone. We share a room so every time he calls, I have to leave or cover my ears. It is getting on my nerves!

Really Annoyed

Dear R.A.,
Can you pool allowances and get a cordless phone so your sister can have privacy and you can have peace? Hang in there. Your sister-to-sister bond will outlast many romances. And before you know it, you, too, may be receiving annoying phone calls!

Dear Carol,
My sister is 12 and she wears eyeliner and is always worrying about her hair. She has been really mean to me. For example, if I'm singing, she'll imitate me or say, "Where did you learn to sing like that, an alien?" Please help. (Mood swing? Preteen age? What?)
Irritated

Dear Irritated,
When she picks on you, are you able to let it go or do you shoot an arrow back at her? What would happen if you said, "I don't feel like fighting, do you?" or even surprised her with a compliment? Fighting fire with water can work. If you can't get her to change her ways, keep reminding yourself that her sarcasm is her problem, not yours.

Dear Carol,
I have an older sister and whenever I have a friend sleep over, the friend wants to hang out with her. My sister gives them makeovers, does their hair, etc. I don't like doing this stuff. I like playing basketball,

*riding bikes, just being outside. I have tried to talk to
my friends, but they never seem to care.*

Taken Over

Dear Taken Over,
Three doesn't have to be a crowd. And most
sleepovers are long enough that there's time for
outdoor and indoor fun with and without third
parties. Some of your friends may even feel lucky
that they get to be with you and also go from
"befores" to "afters." Tell your sister ahead that
after, say, 8:30, you want time alone with your
friend. Promise you'll butt out when her friends
come over. Maybe you could also get your mom
to rent a video or play a game with your sister or
even arrange a sleepover—at someone else's home.

*Dear Carol,
My older sister is a total goody-goody and gets terrific grades. She is also great at sports. She doesn't
care about boys, makeup, and other teenager things.
My mom and dad expect me to be like her. Puh-
leeeeese! The truth is, I stink at sports and get bad
grades, and I'm more interested in teenager stuff. At
my school's open house, my parents and teachers
talked about my sister more than me.*

Can't Be Like Her

Dear C.B.L.H.,
Tell your parents, "I wish you wouldn't compare
me with my sister. I know she's great at school

and sports, but I have different strengths and interests." Then work to develop what makes you you. It's fine to enjoy crushes and cosmetics. But keep up in class, too, and don't give up on finding a sport or activity that you do like. Join the theater crew or student council or the school newspaper and start carving your own niche. It would be ideal if your parents didn't compare you, but you'll feel good when you figure out how to distinguish yourself.

Dear Carol,
I idolize my sister and sometimes I feel like I, too, am 18. I have been through it all: prom, homecoming, boyfriend, turning 16, SATs, and graduation with her. It's strange to think I have to go through it all again myself.

Little Sister

Dear Little Sister,
Strange, perhaps, but I doubt your prom or graduation will feel anticlimactic. It's one thing to be watching your sister grow up, another to be the star of your own home movie.

Dear Carol,
My brother is a jerk. He hits me and puts me down whenever he can. He popped my bean bag and takes my things. He is the oldest and I am the youngest. That means that he can punch me but I can't do anything back because he would cream me. I am afraid

*of him. Shouldn't he stand up for me and be a nice
big brother?*

Pushed Around

Dear Pushed,
Yes. But there are probably as many big-brother
bullies as big-brother protectors. I get a lot of
letters about sibling abuse and I wish I could
suggest a solution that didn't involve months of
family counseling. Talk to your parents or to
another sibling if you think it could help. Tell
your brother, "I wish we could get along." (Can't
hurt.) And next time he's auditioning for the
role of Brother From Hell, don't provoke him, just
stay out of his way. I hope he grows up sooner
instead of later.

*Dear Carol,
My older brother doesn't seem to know I exist. I don't
expect to be best friends, but I want him to see that
I'm not just a little kid. He's always on the phone, in
his room, or out. He used to like being with me.
Sometimes he snaps at me in front of his girlfriends.*

Sad Sis

Dear Sad Sis,
I bet he still likes being with you, even if he
needs more space than ever. You could snap back,
but that won't help. How about taking an opposite tack? Write or say, "I know you like hanging
out with people your age, but I'm here, too, and I

miss you." Suggest going on a hike or to a movie just the two of you. You might even mention that girls like guys who are nice to their siblings. Talk to him and compliment him without being in his face. As you get older, the age gap will seem smaller. And while girlfriends come and go, brothers and sisters are forever.

Dear Carol,
My big sister just got married and I am having trouble dealing with it. We are very close but we have been drifting apart since the wedding bells rang.

Miss My Sis

Dear M.M.S.,
I felt displaced when my brother got married—but I like his wife, and my brother is just a phone call away. It is hard when siblings become wrapped up in new lives. Your sister is in a whirl-wind stage of honeymoon, thank-you notes, and newlywed nest-building. Get busy yourself, then in a month or so, write or call to say how you are happy for her and you like your brother-in-law (if you do) but that you'd love to spend one afternoon just the two of you. Sign it: Miss My Sis. I hope her husband can someday be your friend, too.

Dear Carol,
My sister has already had a baby. She's only 15. She gave the baby to a very older trusted friend. Now

she's pregnant again. She told me never to tell any-
one, including our folks. Should I tell my parents and
have her hate me for the rest of my life, or should I
let nature take its own path?

Confused

Dear Confused,
I'm usually against tattling, but your sister needs
an adult to help her be more responsible with
her life and the lives of others. If nature takes
its course, she won't be able to keep her secret
for long and another baby will be born. Who
will take care of it? Someone has to be thinking about this. Does she intend to have and keep
this baby? Pregnant women need to take extra
good care of their bodies: They need to eat well
and drink milk and take prenatal vitamins and
avoid harmful substances. Your sister can call
Planned Parenthood at 800-230-PLAN to learn
more and she can make important decisions
without parental involvement. Then again, can
your mother guess what's up without your having to spell it out? Might a hint help? Would your
mother's wishes differ from your sister's?

Babies are wonderful for women who are old
enough to take care of them. But most 15-
year-olds still need help taking care of themselves. (You don't always wash your own sheets,
prepare your own dinner, buy soap and cereal
and shoes, and pay the electric bills, do you?) It's

easier to be a happy competent mother if you wait until you're older and are settled, have a job or savings, and ideally, have a loving husband eager to be a father.

Dear Carol,
My 15-year-old sister ran away. I know where she is, but I'm afraid to tell because I don't want to get in trouble.

Confused

Dear Confused,
Some girls rat on siblings to get them in trouble. You'd be speaking up to get her out of trouble. I understand your not wanting to squeal, but think about revealing her whereabouts to a parent, counselor, clergyperson, relative, or some other trusted adult. If she is in danger, you could be saving her life. There's a chance that even she will realize this.

Dear Carol,
I'm afraid my sweet, loving, older brother might have a drug addiction. I was looking for one of my dad's CDs in his room when I found something that I thought looked like weed. I also found cigarettes. I want to tell someone, but I don't know who or what to say. I don't know if I should tell or cover for him. I don't want my brother to die of cancer.

Worried

Dear Worried,

First of all, try not to assume the worst. Everyone who tries drugs is not an addict just as everyone who sips beer is not an alcoholic and everyone who smokes does not die of cancer. That said, I hope he is able to stop now before he ends up in trouble or with lifelong unhealthy habits. If you told your parents, would they overreact—or underreact? Before you confront them, why not tell your brother what you told me? That you love him and are concerned about him. Say that the greedy tobacco companies want him to be a smoker, but you don't. That drugs may seem cool, but they are dangerous. That you don't want to tell your parents but you're worried. You can't change other people. But you can give them information and opinions.

More Sibling Troubles

Dear Carol,

I have a twin sister who is lazy and has a bad attitude about everything. My twin's attitude has made everyone at school mad at her so they think I am exactly like her and they are mad at me also. I want everyone to look at me as me, not my twin.

Problems Of The Identical

Dear P.O.T.I.,

When it comes to look-alike siblings, many kids do say "the twins" instead of "Nicole and

Stephanie" or "Olivia and Angel." If you're weary of being lumped together and considered half a unit instead of one whole person, keep trying to distinguish yourself. Cut your hair or wear it in a signature style so people won't be confused about who's who. Stand out in other ways, too. Instead of taking judo with your sister, sign up for a ceramics course, try out for track, join a youth group, start a once-a-week homework club for kids at a homeless shelter, or spend Tuesday afternoons playing board games with hospitalized children. In other words, figure out who you are and go be that person.

As for your bad-attitude twin, since she's yours forever, think of the big picture and how you (and your family) can help her be a happier person (and better sister). Putting her down won't help—she may already feel outdone by you. Instead, encourage her to build on her strengths and find herself. What does she do when she's not a couch potato? Does she doodle with a cartoonist's hand? Bake delicious brownies? Start praising her. You'll both come out ahead.

Dear Carol,
I have one younger brother and one older sister and I always get blamed for everything because I'm in the middle.

Middle Person

Dear Middle Person,
I bet your younger brother and older sister tell a different story. There are advantages and disadvantages to being older, younger, and in the middle. I hope you can learn to defend yourself politely but firmly when wrongly accused, but also to enjoy your place in your family.

Dear Carol,
My sister is prettier than I am. I know it. I'm not very pretty. Please help.

Bad-Looking Sister

Dear Sister,
Ideally, sisters should think of each other as teammates, not rivals, but sisters often do compete and one sister may have strengths the other does not. Instead of comparing yourself to your sister, become aware of your strengths. Are you friendly? Funny? Artistic? Musical? Great with kids? A runner? Writer? Scientist? Cook? Computer genius? Focus on what you can do and what you enjoy. As for appearance, what makes you attractive is smiling and feeling good about yourself. If you need a boost, get yourself a great haircut or new or vintage clothes. Sometimes a change of style can lead to a change in attitude.

Dear Carol,
My stepsister is always making fun of my body. She even gets my best friend to do it. I sometimes tease

her, too, but not always. Our parents tell us to stop because we'll regret it when we're older. I want to stop but I don't know how.

Fight Prone

Dear Fight Prone,

Say, "I wish we could make a pact to stop being mean to each other. It's gotten to be sort of a habit." Something like that? Speak to your best friend, too. Anyone who makes fun of your body is insecure about her own.

Dear Carol,

My parents are divorced and I have a 13-year-old stepsister who is one month younger than me. My stepmom always compares my mistakes to her perfectness. For example, "Well, your sister has a lot of friends, why don't you?" I try to tell her I'm not like my stepsister, I'm ME, but she doesn't get it.

Not Perfect

Dear N.P.,

No one's perfect and pooh on your stepmom for putting you down. Can you ask your dad for help? Or even your stepsister? Tell your stepmother that you and your stepsister have separate gifts and goals and that the constant comparing is undermining your confidence—which doesn't help anything.

Dear Carol,

I have a sister who has mental problems. She has had counseling and still needs help. I try to be strong for her like my parents asked me to, but sometimes even though she doesn't mean to, she scares me. I don't know how to help her.

Helping?

Dear Helping?,

I'm sure you are helping her by just being you. Be as honest to your parents as you were in your letter. Tell them that you sometimes feel scared. I think they will understand and have some ideas for you.

Dear Carol,

I'm at the end of my strings with my brother's girl-friend. She is such a suck-up to my family that it's unbelievable. It seems they all like her much more than me. My parents say I'm jealous, which is not true at all. She is stealing my brother away from me, and I want to sock her in the nose.

Holding On Tightly

Dear Holding On Tightly,

If you were at your boyfriend's, you'd be on your best behavior and would be hoping to befriend your boyfriend's sister, not replace her. Right? This girl isn't your archenemy. Can you relax and make friends with her instead of imagining that your family has to choose between you? They aren't being disloyal to you—they're being nice to her. They still love you and will long after she's been replaced by the next girlfriend and the next. If you miss your brother, tell him, e-mail him, or put a note under his door. Sometimes it can be easier to write, "Hey I miss you!" than to say it.

Dear Carol,
My parents are divorced and my mom remarried a guy with a fat, annoying, nose-picking 5-year-old son and an adorable 13-year-old son. I hate the 5-year-old and his dad, but I have a crush on the older kid. My friends and mom love the 5-year-old. Help! I'm losing attention!

Grossed Out And Brother Crazy

Dear Grossed Out And Brother Crazy,
Blended families aren't easy, but give things time. The little guy will learn not to pick his nose, and with a nudge, your mom will remember to dote on you. You're also going to feel better if you can get along with your stepdad. You hate him? Dig deeper. Find something tolerable about him. Now about that adorable stepbro . . . as you know, things would get weird if you two became an item. You may not be blood relatives, but you are stepsiblings. Enjoy the natural feelings that are sparking between you, but think friendship, not romance. If you handle this well, you can be friends for life.

Dear Carol,
My brother has a calendar on his wall of women in bikinis and lingerie. It makes me feel uncomfortable, and I'm afraid to have friends over because they might see it. I can't ask my brother to take it down because he wouldn't listen.

Oh Brother

Dear Oh Brother,
Your brother is not the only one with a sexy calendar and your friends won't hold it against you. (This is America. They've seen it all already.) Invite them over and rest assured that they also feel uncomfortable about how loudly their parents fight or how much their big brother swears or little sister tags along. By the way, in case you've been doing any comparing, real women rarely look like pin-ups.

Dear Carol,
My older brother gets on-line a lot and goes into chat rooms. One day he left the computer on and I wanted to get on and I saw everything he and his friends said. They cussed, talked about sick things, and my brother said he hated our parents. I know I shouldn't have looked, but now I don't know what to do with this information.

Help!

Dear Help!,
Let it go. If you found out that your brother, God

forbid, was hiring a hit man, you'd have to take action. But you've found out that, among his male friends, he curses and is lewd and sometimes trashes a pair of perfectly nice parents. That may not be admirable, but it's not illegal or even all that unusual. His relationship with your parents is changing but not ending, and his scorn of them now may help him figure out who he is and how he is different from them. My two older brothers sometimes got impatient with our parents, but after those trying years, we all managed to get along well again. (Most of the time anyway!)

Dear Carol,
My family and I want to get a dog, but my sister is afraid of them. She did say she is starting to get used to them, but I don't think I can wait until she is totally ready.

Waiting

Dear Waiting,
Head to the library and learn about different kinds of dogs. Some dogs may seem scary to your sister (e.g. Dobermans or pit bulls) and others may make her melt (e.g. Shih Tzus or golden retrievers). If she alone is holding this up, maybe your family can let your sister pick the breed or name the dog. Involve your sister in the dog decision, and who knows? She may be ready tomorrow.

Dear Carol,
My brother always steals my money. I put it in a wal-
let in a drawer, but he keeps coming in to my room
and taking it. At first, it was just a dollar or two, but
last week he took twenty dollars from me. I con-
fronted him but he couldn't even look me in the eye
and say he didn't do it. I don't know where to keep
my money. My parents have a safe but I don't know
the combination.

Annoyed

Dear Annoyed,
Forget wallets and piggy banks; put your money
in a boot at the top of your closet or in a book
he'd never open or behind your flowered stationery. (I'm assuming your parents don't spring-
clean your room without asking first.) And warn
your brother that if he steals again, you'll tell
your parents.

Dear Carol,
My mom and my 15-year-old brother do not get
along. They fight day and night. He's practically
ruined our lives!

Why Me?

Dear Why Me?,
While many families are warm and loving, others are boiling over. Can your mother and brother
get professional counseling? Can you suggest this?
Family therapy may seem expensive, but peace is

priceless. For now, their wars don't have to ruin your life. Enjoy friends, do well in school, and walk away when they go at it. Before you know it, your brother will be off to college or out on his own. Meantime, if you're ever tempted to say something nice to or about your brother, do so! He may feel the whole family is against him, and knowing you care could make a difference.

Dear Carol,
I'm going out with a guy, but I think my sister likes him. She talks to him on the phone a lot. And I think he likes her! Should I dump him and let my sister be happy?

Boyfriend And Sister Trouble

Dear Boyfriend And Sister Trouble,
No. Chances are your boyfriend is a good guy and your sister feels comfortable with him. So they are enjoying each other's company and maybe even flirting a little. That doesn't mean you should back off. Unless you've gotten tired of the guy, I'd mention to both (separately) that you are glad they get along but you feel a little uneasy when they hang out on the phone. Confess to your sister that you're insecure and you want her to respect your romance. Voice your concerns to your boyfriend, too—he may rush to reassure you that you're the one he cares about.

Dear Carol,
Help! I'm falling for my sister's boyfriend.
Can't Break It To Her

Dear C.B.I.T.H.,
How many nice guys are there? How many sisters do you have? Your relationship with your sister will last your whole life. Don't jeopardize it for what would probably be a short-lived romance. Tell yourself, "Don't go there," and let the sparks between you and him turn into embers instead of flames. Respect her turf, and let's hope she never steps between you and someone you care about.

Dear Carol,
I have a serious problem. My parents want to adopt a Chinese girl. I really don't want to because I think it will change my life too drastically. I like my life the way it is. Could you give me some advice on how to deal with the new baby if we adopt one? Thanks.
Against Adopting

Dear A.A.,
While adopting a baby is a huge step, you may end up liking life even more as a sister. At first you may feel mad or jealous, as well as excited. But soon you may get a kick out of having a little sister who lights up when you approach and struggles to say your name and reaches for your hand. She'll annoy you sometimes, but she'll

also add more love to your life. And what a difference your parents and you are making in hers!

Advice? Try to be honest with your parents, and encourage them to be honest, too. If you say, "Mom, I like my life so I'm nervous about our plans," and she says, "Nonsense, it'll be wonderful," say, "I know, but aren't you a little nervous, too?" Really talk. It's better to acknowledge and prepare for the difficulties of adding a baby (adopted or not) to the household rather than to pretend things will be hunky-dory, then be disappointed when the baby cries a lot or you feel left out. But be positive, too. You have big-hearted parents who enjoy being parents. And you're going to have a sister to laugh with and love.

Dear Carol,
When I was little, my brother, who is six years older than I am, would have me take off my clothes and would feel my private areas. I've forgiven him, but I've had three boyfriends and each one of them I dumped because they were pressuring me to kiss them. I'm so afraid to get close to a guy in that way. I've only told a few friends, and no one knows it was my brother. I can't tell my mom—she is so proud of her son. I'm boy-crazy, but once I get the boy, I totally freak out. I love my brother, but this is affecting my love life.

Confused

Dear Confused,

I'm sorry your brother took liberties with you and that you can't tell your mother. No wonder you feel confused! Your past and present are indeed connected. You may have forgiven your brother for taking advantage of you, but inside the understanding-preteen you is a little-girl you who is still (understandably!) upset. I hope you can find a good therapist to help you sort through this. Many girls feel both boy-crazy and freaked-out, but you're smart to recognize that in your case, there's more going on. Open up to a guidance counselor or trusted adult. Someday you will welcome a boyfriend's kiss. But it's very wise to wait until you're ready.

Relatively Speaking

Dear Carol,
My parents are both divorced and remarried. I live with my grandparents. People always say I'm rich or lucky. They live with both their parents though. No one believes me when I say they're lucky. I say love is better. Still nobody listens.

Hurt In The Heart

Dear Hurt,
They are trying to make you feel better. But you want to be listened to, not cheered up. Your situation is hard. Are you able to see, call, or write your parents? Is either of them able to express

love for you? Let your grandparents know how much you appreciate them, but try to talk with them about your feelings, too. Lots of people aren't good listeners, but someone out there is: a new friend? Girl Scout leader? school nurse?

Dear Carol,
My grandma says mean things about my dad ever since my mom (her daughter) died. What should I do?
Confused

Dear Confused,
Say, "Grandma, I miss Mom, too, but don't you think it's good that I love my dad? I wish you wouldn't talk about him that way."

Dear Carol,
My parents and grandparents have been feuding for six years, and I haven't been allowed to see my grandparents. I've tried talking to my parents, but they get mad. I've tried talking to my grandparents, but they don't know what they did. Will someone tell me what's going on?
Feud Fright

Dear Feud Fright,
In Judy Blume's *Are You There God? It's Me, Margaret*, the girl's mom is feuding with her parents, too. While family feuds are common, it's awful when kids lose out because of adult

arguments. Your parents may someday tell you what's up or may even end the cold war. Perhaps your grandparents are better at being grandparents than they were at being parents and your parent is still hurting from old wounds. You may not be able to get everyone to kiss and make up, but if you are allowed to phone or write or e-mail, don't hold back.

Dear Carol,
My grandmother moved in with us a few years ago. She does crazy things in front of my friends, and I get embarrassed. How do I tell her to cool it?
                                                    Not Amused

Dear Not Amused,
Kids often feel embarrassed by parents or relatives. If friends think your grandmother is kooky, it won't make them think less of you. If your grandmom is whistling while eating pickled herring, give her a break. If she's wearing underwear on her head, talk to your parents. Be aware of your grandmother's feelings, though. Most people have many friends in a lifetime, but only one or two grandmoms (maybe a few more in blended families).

Dear Carol,
My family just found out that my grandma has cancer in a lot of different places. Now she is taking pills

to help slow down the cancer. I'm afraid she won't live long enough to see me grow up to be a fine citizen. What should I do to make my times with her more special? What should I do to be strong about this?

Upset

Dear Upset,
Call and write more often than usual. Send her drawings, cards, schoolwork, photos. Say, "I love you," a lot. Talk with your parents—they're probably sad, too. If they approve, ask your grandmother to tell you her favorite stories or recipes or memories. Consider writing or videotaping her. Try not to sob in front of her, but if you do cry or mist up, forgive yourself. It would just show how much you love her. And don't wait to become a fine citizen; do what you can now.

Dear Carol,
My grandmother died last month. We were close and we baked cookies together and she even taught me to speak a little Russian. I loved her a lot and I miss her. My mom seems sad, too, but we never talk about it. I wouldn't know what to say.

Sad

Dear Sad,
Say, "I miss Grandmom, don't you?" Your mom might appreciate being able to remember her mother aloud and knowing that you, like her,

have happy memories. Even if your mother cries, don't think you are making her sadder. She may already be sad, and it will be nice for both of you to grieve together instead of separately. You can also bake those cookies and know that, in some ways, your grandmother will always be with you. I'm sure she loved you as much as you loved her.

Dear Carol,
My grandma died two years ago. My grandpa got married again. I don't know if I should call her by her first name or "Grandma."

Confused

Dear Confused,
If she hasn't stated a preference, it's up to you. If you don't feel comfortable using her name or calling her "Grandma," consider a word like *Nana* or *Grandmother*. You could also ask her or your grandpa to decide this with you. Do decide though because your thank-you notes to them shouldn't start with "Hey, you!"

Dear Carol,
My aunt died of a stupid disease called breast cancer. She had a 2-year-old son. It makes me sad because he shouts, "Mommy!" every time he looks at me because I look like his mom. I feel like holding him and telling him I am his mommy, but I can't. I miss her so much, and I can't forget her.

Can't Forget

Dear Can't Forget,
What a tragic loss for you and your cousin.
You're right: You can't say you are his mommy.
But you can hold him and say you miss his
mommy, too, and that you loved her and that you
love him.

Dear Carol,
I have a cousin who is always over at my house.
Constantly. No kidding. I'm going crazy. His dad is in
jail because he was caught selling drugs. My cousin
cries a lot and is extremely jealous of me.
                                        Sick And Tired Of It

Dear Sick And Tired Of It,
I can see why you're tired of him . . . but I can see
why he's unhappy, too. If he were a pesky neighbor, it would be one thing, but since he's family
and in need, you may just have to put up with his
visits. Talk to your parents. Don't feel you always
have to get out the Legos or join him in front
of a computer game. But do consider his point of
view. Having a father in jail is harder than having an annoying cousin.

Dear Carol,
I have a cousin who always makes me and my sister
do bad things, and she comes over every Saturday.
Today in our car, she made us moon people as they
went by in their cars and trucks. She's done even

worse things in the past, and I'm sure there are more bad things in the future. Help!

Desperate

Dear Desperate,
Now wait a second. She makes you do bad things? Unless she's armed, she can't *make* you do bad things, because you can say no. Use your best judgment instead of following wacky suggestions. Start saying no. Tell her you like her but don't like getting in trouble. If her visits continue to cause problems, ask your parents for help. And on the interstate, keep your pants on!

Dear Carol,
During dinner over vacation, I went to the bathroom and found my 7-year-old cousin crying. She had had an accident in her pants and didn't want her mother to find out. I got the impression that this wasn't the first time, and she said that her mother gets really mad and punishes her. I gave my cousin a pair of my sister's panties. We got done just in time because her mother was coming down the hall. I said that my cousin had a stomachache. Now I wonder if I did the right thing. I don't like lying to my aunt, but I don't want to get my cousin in trouble either. But maybe at her age, she does deserve to be punished for wetting her pants. I overheard once that she wets her bed, too. What do you think?

Concerned Cousin

Dear C.C.,

I think you did fine. Your cousin needs compassion, not punishment, and that's what you gave her. Some kids have accidents and wet their beds more than other kids. The problem even has a name—enuresis—and it's genetic, which means the parents may have had the same troubles. Your cousin will probably grow out of it, and may want to consult her doctor, but in the meantime, her mom's anger may be hurting more than helping. Can you discuss this with your mother?

Dear Carol,

I have three cousins. One is 5, one is 2, and one is a newborn. I try to give them all equal attention, but since the newborn is so cute, I want to hold her a lot. The 2-year-old always wants to play house, and the 5-year-old wants to play board games. I just can't give them all equal attention.

Can't Do It

Dear Can't,

Those kids are lucky to have a cousin who loves them, so don't feel guilty that you can't do the impossible. Instead of trying to give each cousin equal time, try to give each some special time. Perhaps you can also hold the baby while singing to the 2-year-old. Or play house with both the toddler and 5-year-old. Lots of moms and dads find it hard to give enough time to their kids, and I hope your aunt and uncle appreciate your help and enthusiasm. Sounds like you're a wonderful cousin—and I bet you'd be an ideal baby-sitter.

The End

Whether you finished this whole book or just dipped into it, whether you're returning it to a friend, library, or your own shelf, I thank you for joining me here on page 344. And I invite you to come back if you ever have a blowout with your dad, an impossible unshakable crush, a friend who acts weird about eating, a mortifyingly personal question, or if you ever just feel stumped.

I'm here if you need me; and, while I had plenty of was-my-face-red moments back in school, I usually have a pretty good handle on things now. So remember, when you're full of questions, this book is full of answers. And when you're feeling low, there is always somebody nearby to turn to—a parent, godparent, relative, teacher, coach, counselor, member of the clergy, nurse, doctor, social worker, neighbor, *somebody*. You aren't alone. You really aren't.

For now, though, I guess this is good-bye.

Be smart. Be kind. Take care of yourself.

I'm on your side, and I don't want you to feel sad, mad, hurt, annoyed, upset, scared, confused, or embarrassed—let alone clueless, desperate, ashamed, or abnormal.

My real hope is that you're beginning to feel not just normal, but strong, confident, and ready for takeoff.

You are?

Excellent!

Then pick up some speed.
On your mark . . . get set . . . go!
Yes! That's it!
You're flying!
Now stay on course and give it all you've got!
I'm wishing you good luck all the way.

Love,

Carol Weston

Carol Weston

Who's Dear Carol Anyway?

Although Carol Weston was born in the last century, she isn't thaaat old. Carol is the advice columnist for *Girls' Life* Magazine and the author of *Girltalk: All the Stuff Your Sister Never Told You* and *For Girls Only: Wise Words, Good Advice*. Both books are out in Chinese. Carol does not speak Chinese but she does speak French and Spanish, and was graduated summa cum laude from Yale University with a degree in French and Spanish literature. She also has an M.A. from Middlebury College.

Carol has appeared on *The View* and has been a guest of Oprah, Montel, Ricki, Geraldo, and Sally. She's written for *Seventeen*, *Teen*, *YM*, *Parents*, *Redbook*, *Family Circle*, and *Glamour*, and has done author chats on Yahoo and ivillage. Her first novel is *The Diary of Melanie Martin*. Carol lives in Manhattan with her husband and two daughters and their rabbit, Honey Bunny. Carol enjoys being a girl even though she's a grown-up.